MANNA FROM HEAVEN

SHANE W ROESSIGER

H.O.T. House of Truth – Apostolic Center

360 S Tamiami Trail – Nokomis – FL – (941) 412-5414

Equipping the Saints – Sending them out

www.hothouseoftruth.com

BREAKING BREAD

"Give us today our daily bread."

Matthew 6:11

PERFECTING FAITH

In the Kingdom of God, everything is empowered by faith. Let us hold fast the profession of our faith. The profession of our faith pleases Him. Whether you see it or not, believe that He is faithful. The ones that did not follow the law of Moses died in the wilderness. So now we that have received the power of faith, He will judge us as well.

Live by the promises you cannot see. Cast not away your confidence on the cross, your faith in His faithfulness, and your faith in what you were called to do. The just shall always live by faith. He wants our faith to be perfected in us, walking by faith, not feelings. We live by what we believe. We live by what is said, not by what it looks like or by what it feels like. Our faith is constantly being tried.

He has told us things through the pages of His Word, but also, He has told us personal things. By patience, we need to keep hold of those things we heard from Him. Obey Him even when you don't feel like it.

The unjust will live by what they see, but the just will live by faith.

People ask: "God, show me what to do, where to go?" but God is saying, "I already told you." What are you going to do with what He already told you? Without faith, we cannot please Him and to please Him is why and what we live for. Everyone has a deep yearning to please God. The Bible tells us that it is our faith that pleases Him.

Faith is the evidence of things not seen. My walk is justified by my faith. One thing is to be justified by what He did, but also, it is important to be justified by our own faith. It is important to obey Him because that proves our faith in what He did. Even everything seen was not created by what was seen. That which was not seen was spoken and caused things to be created! Everything starts with faith and ends with faith.

Enoch believed God and His reward was to be translated. We should not do things because of the reward but because of faith. When our faith is perfected, it does not matter what is going on around us. Our faith is the most valuable thing we have. It moves heaven and earth. Live your life according to your faith whether people call you a fool or not, whether you look ridiculous or not. Great men of faith were mocked and ridiculed in their time, but now they are being talked about almost every day by someone (**Hebrews 12**).

Are you going to have a good report through to inherit the promises? That is why we have to go from faith to faith and not from faith to fear. Faith will help you to get through, and if you don't have it, your boat will be shaken. The enemy would love to steal your faith.

God is perfecting faith in us so we can stand! Lay aside every sin of unbelief!!! This is the greatest sin that will stop us from entering into His promised land! He is the master of all faith. We don't have to have faith in ourselves but in Him!

Quit looking at you in the mirror! Look unto Jesus, the author and the finisher of our faith. He endured the cross. We need to endure ours and our faith will be perfected. What proceeds out of the great chapter of faith is what God does.

There is an IF. If you endure the chastisement, you are His son. We need to be subjected to our Father in the Spirit – GOD – and then we will live. Whether it gets monotonous or not, we still need to keep going and doing what He called us to do. Then you will please our Father! Because if you need Him to show up every time you do something for Him, that is not faith, and you are not even pleasing Him! When you keep doing what needs to be done even when you don't see the result, that proves your faith. What keeps you from falling out of grace? Faith! The kingdom of faith is the only kingdom that will not and cannot be shaken.

Whoever said that being led by the Spirit of God is only feelings? Sometimes the feeling stops because God is testing if you will do what He told you in spite of your feelings. The kingdom of God is not by observation or feelings. What releases heaven is your faith. Your faith will make you whole. Faith will sanctify you!

There are a lot of days that we don't feel like doing anything, and you start counting the cost, but Jesus is not looking for yesterday's yes. Will He find faith? Or find you doing it? Jesus said: "Will I find faith in you when I come," and He continues with saying "find you doing." Faith has works!

Sometimes you don't see wisdom, but suddenly you start acting more wisely because you asked for it in faith. There are evidences of our faith now and others will manifest in the future. It is not just the asking part that is important. It is the asking in faith! How can you recognize a man full of faith? By his actions! Let faith motivate your do!

Honor those who are rich in faith. They are the heirs of His kingdom. Faith perfects everything in us concerning the Kingdom of God. Saying what you believe does not prove what you believe. Faith without works is dead. How to perfect our faith? By works. By doing it. **James 2:22**

Your faith will make you a friend of God. How do you get to that place? Increase your faith. We need to have living faith and act on it. According to our faith, it will be done unto us all. What do you believe for? It will be done by faith. That is the evidence. Everybody says, "I believe," but they really don't because there is no evidence! When we really believe, we do! When we do, then it is faith!

We need to see the evidence of our faith! Even the apostles asked, "Increase my faith." Don't stay where you are. God wants an ever-increasing faith. Jesus prayed for Peter that his faith would not fail. We need to strengthen ourselves and one another. That is why the scripture says, "Do not forsake togetherness."

Faith not only saves you but sanctifies you. Keep doing it. Keep moving in it. Love and obey Him all the time. Make an effort. I will do the right thing today because it will matter tomorrow. Everything in the world is for today, but in the kingdom of faith, it is all about tomorrow. It is our faith in Him that we need to master, not in ourselves.

The righteousness of God is revealed from faith to faith, and as it is written: THE JUST SHALL LIVE BY FAITH! The hearers of the Word hear about it, but only the doers of the Word obtain His promises. Let us do all that faith asks and pleases God because that is what we are living for!

BREAKING BREAD

Hebrews 10:14-29, Hebrews 11, James 1, James 2, Matthew 9, Romans 1:16-17

{

Some have gone so far down a slippery slope that some ministers are saying that preaching the Word of God is beating up the sheep! I heard this years ago, and it made my skin crawl. Those who are called to preach the Gospel and now are the ones who dull the sword of God to be liked or followed will be called wicked in the day of the Lord. What ends up happening is that they start to preach about themselves. God is raising Elijah prophets, not soothsayers.

....

If God shows you a stumbling block in your life, and you stop at them but don't stumble, that is called a distraction. God shows us things so we can remove them out of our way. When we give an ear to stumbling blocks, we are giving our time. This is why the Father spoke about dusting our feet. Why? Because there are souls waiting and those who will hear you and need what you have to say. It's time to do some dusting. I am dusting my feet in love.

TRUTH: CAN YOU EAT IT?

The Old Testament is for new believers to see Jesus and to walk in the liberty that He has called us to. If you don't see Him in everything you read, then I question if you know Him. The system of that time was just like the system now. They had the Word but some saw Him, some did not see Him, and some said they saw but they were blind. Those remained blind. Jesus said, "Since you say you see, you will remain blind." Blind pride is what I am talking about.

You might know the scripture or verse but does scripture or the verse know you? Jesus came for many reasons, but He came for reasons. The one that changed the world was truth, mercy, and love. I warn you, if you take the old and mix it with the new you are asking to be put back in bondage. Trying to mix the law and grace is like trying to mix oil and water! We are sons and daughters of the free woman, not of the bondwoman! Read **Galatians 4, 5, and 6**. Don't let anyone entangle you! A little leaven leavens the whole lump! Everything we need is in Christ! I'm seeing so many being pulled down into low-level Christianity by mixing covenants. A double minded man keeps the law and tries to walk in grace, but it's not going to happen! The law could not do what grace does: perfect love. Do I become your enemy because I tell you the truth? Even Paul, he would rather have you been separated from them because if you did not, they would eventually exclude you because some people cannot wrap their minds around freedom. Freedom is not pagan. Freedom is not a list of do's and don'ts! Freedom is dying to self and full submission to the power of God perfecting us in righteousness by His Grace! Freedom is not lawlessness. It is full OBEDIENCE to the Holy Spirit! Flesh profits nothing, meaning I cannot do anything apart from God and God is Spirit. God did not write the New Testament to be a secret mystery to you! These were believers being persecuted, burned alive, and decapitated for their faith! Paul cries: Stop trying to be a Jew. Stop trying to observe things! Stop the works of the flesh! Come into a higher level of sonship. Grace is a higher level than the curse – by it we cry, Abba Father!

These things are causing division because those who have tasted freedom in Christ hear God and will die before they get yoked to bondage again. My God! Jesus took the needle out my arm not to preach the old letter and its Jewish roots and traditions! It was so I can preach Christ, Him crucified and resurrected! The cross means nothing to those who are perishing, but to us who believe, it is the power of God! If He did not rise from the dead, it's all worthless! There is no power in knowledge. There is no reward in observing the letter! We are justified by faith and without it, it's impossible to please Him! Get it! Stop causing confusion. Repent, for the kingdom of God is at hand! Grace is the power to become the sons of God! The law is fulfilled in Truth, grace, and love. Bind it around your neck, Brethren! Walk in your new creation status and take your city! I am pleading for your life! You will die in the letter! But we are redeemed from the curse of it, PRAISE THE LORD!

THE GOVERMENT OF GOD

Until we submit to His Government (I'm not talking about religious institutions and dead works), we won't be anything but lone rangers! This is so interesting! Mark my words! God is shutting down itinerant ministry. It's not biblical! Individualism was old covenant priesthood. We are now in Body ministry! Glory comes from submission to one another and Godly order! The body cannot function if it is in parts. It must be connected! We are not to separate ourselves from ourselves. We are His body! Apart from that, you're just a gift with no authority or power. If we are one Body, we are one with Christ. In Him, we breathe and move! We have a covenant with Him. When we break out of covenant with the body (brothers and sisters), we are breaking covenant with Him, period. Religion will always cut the body apart. It's a spirit of division, separation and murder. It's anti-Christ. When we don't submit to the Body, we are not submitting to Christ! This is where **John chapter 17** comes in. It's Christ in us, the Glory of God! So, we are submitting to Christ in one another, NOT TO MAN! We are one in Spirit. God is spirit. That's the Truth. We cannot separate ourselves from ourselves unless we are not of Christ.

All have different parts. God is a God of order, and He is the head of the Body. We are different parts of one body, so submitting to one another is submitting to Jesus! We are one in the Spirit! It's His Spirit that makes the Body move so God is Spirit. We are led by that spirit. Until we realize that, we will not move in the Spirit. So, when we don't submit to mantles (vision from God) and government, it's not man we reject. It's Christ we reject. Remember when Jesus said shake and dust off? It means they are rejecting. Don't ever let religion cut your lifeline off. It's a root of pride.

{ God told me that people always need to find something to make themselves feel worthy when all He wants is for us to believe in His power! When we try to do more to please Him, it births religion. Because He did so much, it actually hurts Him. Man always wants to take credit! It's like trying to do more because you want to boast. He is making us HOLY. He is making us dead to this world by the working on our surrendering to His power of transformation from glory to glory! He is an all-consuming fire. Let Him consume us! Let Him shake everything that can be shaken. He is doing work in us when we submit to His will and His word, and daily searching ourselves, judging ourselves, and obeying Him. His sheep hear Him. Do not let man tell you that He ONLY speaks through the letter. He uses the letter to confirm what the Spirit is saying to you and using the Spirit to see what He is saying in the letter. We need both. He said my words are spirit. They are life. Eat His flesh; drink His blood. He never calls us to go on a diet. Don't let man try to lead you by letter only. You will be in the ditch. In no time, we are bankrupt without His Spirit! Believe me, staying in the Spirit takes a lot of dying. If you want to work on something, work on submission!

"Day by day continuing with one mind in the temple, and breaking bread from house to house, they were taking their meals together with gladness and sincerity of heart."

Acts 2:46

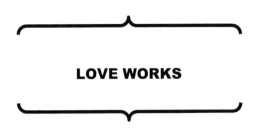

LOVE WORKS

If I speak in tongues...and if I have the gift of prophecy...and if I have revelation...The word of **1 Corinthians 13** is a direct word to those filled with the Spirit. You can be doing works of justice, give to the poor, but still not walk in love, in the character of God's heart. You can see, you can give your body for religion, but not be in love. Paul completely just lays it down. Love has all to do with the edifying of another. Basically, it is selfless love.

Love has no rights. When you want to be right, want to be heard, want to have it your way, that is not love. You can't truly love until you are truly dead. You have to fight to do the opposite. If you don't abide in Him, you will not be able to manifest the kingdom of God.

Faith. Hope. Love. The three cords that will preserve us until the end. They are not just about gifts. When we move in the gifts in love, the kingdom of God will manifest.

A peacemaker is not the one that pleases man. It is a man that speaks Truth in love but avoids the conflict that comes from argumentative reasoning. Bless those that curse you, pray for those who misuse you, and keep walking in love. When you are persecuted for doing right, you are blessed. Even when you are right, you don't have to try to prove you are right. Then love is dying because you are now defending you. Love does not do that either.

How are we going to love the World rightly? We all have to come to the same measure of love. He will use anything around you to perfect love in you. You keep putting away childish things. Then you become like a mature man in Christ. So, Paul was saying, "When I was a child, I acted like it, but when love is manifesting that means that God has raised me up." If I do not allow Him to be perfected in me, I stay as a child.

Remember: you can lose your saltiness. How? By falling out of love. Put some salt (love) in the Truth you speak and in the things you do, but speak Truth. Without love, Paul and Jesus say, it will profit nothing! Paul was not accepted by the disciples for years during His conversion time! People backstabbed him, left him, and spoke against him, but he decided to walk in love beside them all. Then he had the world looking for him, arresting him, and persecuting him. He saw the power of love. He saw the kingdom of God manifest time and time again.

Bind mercy and Truth and grace around your neck. The woman caught in adultery found mercy in Jesus. Truth, grace, and mercy met her that day. She first met with Truth and condemnation at the same time. She felt hopeless and condemned then suddenly she looked up and found the Truth, grace, and mercy. She found love. She found forgiveness. She received it. She still knew she was guilty, but her life was saved and changed. Truth and mercy told her: "Sin no more."

If your light goes out, even though you might have the Holy Spirit, nobody will see Christ in you. Love in the world always has a hidden agenda. The whole agenda is to advance their own kingdoms and selfish motives, but it is not the love of God. You don't give love because you get love back. You give love because it is His commandment. We freely receive. We must freely give.

Jesus did not go around seeking attention. He got attention, on the cross! When we love purely, we receive everything purely from the Father. He got attention when He rose from the dead. He got attention, not because His heart was seeking it, but because He was love.

You don't need to recite the Ten commandments because love never breaks them. We can be in danger of judgment if we don't walk in love. Leave your gift at the altar and reconcile with your brother or God won't receive you. People are still mad at their father or mother for years and still go to the altar like it never happened. We want to see God when we preach, or when we do this and that, but we won't if we are not walking in love. So, make it right as soon as possible. We can be put in spiritual prison if we don't walk in love. Satan has dominion to speak in your heart and mind because of that. It becomes rebellion. It is demonic! He will use offended people to attack others that don't even know about their hurt. Most people don't ever know they offended another person until they start to see them. Satan takes territory in Christians if they don't obey the Word of God. It is all about us going back to the cross! Doing that, He will always accept us. The cross is where we die and He lives. People who focus on the commandments are Pharisees and Sadducees. Why? Because Jesus, time and time again, said all the commandments hang on these two: Love God with all your heart, and love your neighbor as yourself. So, focus on God. He is love. What He is saying is that if love is perfected in you, you are fulfilling and obeying all the commandments. So, the Kingdom of God hangs on love. Let the Holy Spirit perfect this in you and you will manifest God on the Earth, and you will be perfect.

If we get offended and don't repent, Satan will start using us. He is the father of lies. God does not want a civil war in the Body of Christ. Satan will take you out and turn you over to his kingdom. His kingdom is darkness with no salt. If you keep focusing on the commandments, Jesus said – you will not be able to keep them. You perfect love and you will be perfected. He was not abolishing the commandments. He was showing us how we can actually be perfect.

People will turn on you, but you can't turn on God. Love works. If people allow offense and evil thoughts, you will become victims of hate! So, love them and let them go. If your brother hits you, don't hit back. Turn away. Don't pay evil for evil. Repay evil with love. You will see heaven and earth moving. You will see so many turning to Jesus. Is that not our assignment? We are all called into that ministry called reconciliation.

Jesus always put people's focus on the little children. Why? Little kids love perfectly. They don't hold offense. They have not been poisoned by the world. They may fight one minute and the next minute they are playing again. This is our prayer. That we will love like them. You can never hear enough about love. Jesus said this is what my kingdom looks like. Study kids' behavior: they don't worry about food or clothes. They are just playing without a care. Their entire dependency for their needs is on mom and dad. They know they got it covered. Be perfect in this love! Be like these little ones.

Then you have the rich young ruler who kept His commandments (Law) but lacked one thing: love! Jesus wanted His love to be perfected in him. He wanted his trust in the world to be replaced by the trust in the kingdom of God. Yep. You are self-righteous. You lack one thing " Sell all you have and give all away and follow Me, totally abandoned to love." He went away sad that day. If he had a good heart, and it was good ground and he got the word, who knows what that man did weeks or years later.

Your heart will always accept love or reject it. It will receive, change, or will reject it. We need to say NO to temptation and run to Him. The enemy will cause you to believe that you don't have to, but you need to run for your life! One that has been forgiven much loves much! Sometimes we think, "We are good," and Jesus is saying, "No one is good, not even Myself. There is only one good! The Father who is in heaven!" What He was saying is this: until you die, you are always being perfected.

God does not say that good is enough. He says, "Be perfect just as I am!"

In your heart, you need to take that low place even if you are right. Jesus was killing them with love, mercy, and Truth. They dropped the stones, they left mad, but He told the woman to sin no more. He did not say, "You just broke the law, number so and so." But all the law hangs on love. That is why it is the first commandment. We know He was talking about the Ten Commandments that Moses got on the mountain because He said it. Religious people make it look like a big mystery, a list of commandments secretly in the Torah. Nope, there are Ten – more than ten now, but if you perfect love, you will fulfill them all.

Everybody wants God to tell them what to do, what commandment to obey. When it is really clear: to LOVE GOD and your NEIGHBORS. Why are they in the first two on t? Because if you do these two things, you will never break any of the commandments. Everyone wants to go back to the law because the law is easier than perfection, but the law is low level. Love is the most excellent one. Love is the Truth. Love is the way. Love is the life and that is who God is – love.

My little children, sin no more, but if you sin, there is an advocate always available. Love will always answer the humble. Love will always resist the proud.

If you say I love Him and don't love brothers and sisters, you are a liar and the Truth (love) is not in you. The Truth can leave you and your conscience is seared. Some people could hold the Truth years ago but today may be in error. Error comes later because of lust! We need to be baptized in the fear of the Lord so love can be perfected. Love keeps and obeys the commandments. Grace is higher level. In the law, you have rights. In grace and love, you have none. You can't even look at a woman, forget about touching her. His perfection is His commandment.

Every man that has this hope purifies themselves. The World loves its own. That is why many places are full of error. They say nice things but not the Truth. Always having a smile on your face is not love. Only God's love is real. We are not supposed to love in words, but to love in deed and in Truth. According to our master and teacher, there is a worldly love that is false. False love. False peace. False unity. False and anti-Christ. Anti-love.

When we love His way, we know that He abides in us. Let us love one another because anyone that loves God is born of God. God is love. He perfected love on Earth through Jesus. Now Jesus is within you. Jesus brought even His feelings under submission to the Word of God. He said if you love me, you will obey my commandments. Start with the first one, and when that is fulfilled, then you are perfect!

We are supposed to do the same. Bring everything under submission so love can flow out of us.

If you don't walk in love, you can't access anything in heaven. When we go to the cross because of love, the love of God is perfected in us. If you don't put His word above yourself, your feelings, or your rights, His love is not in you. If you say you love

God and don't love your brother, then the love of God is not in you. How can we say we love what we don't see when we can't even love our brother or sister that we do see? You are losing the God in you because you are cutting off God in your brother.

Let love be perfected in you. If we can love our enemies first, everything else will be easier. Go for the hardest love. First love your enemies and loving your brothers and sisters will be easier! In the book of Acts, look at the life of Stephen. That God kind of love was perfected in Him and fast. Let's perfect this love with one another.

Love does work. Let it work in us every single day. Help us, Father, to love you and one another more than ever! For what is to come, we need to decide to love with God's love more than ever! The love of God will pour out more than ever! The New Covenant is the covenant of love and death to self, a covenant of a pure heart, a covenant of pure love. Let us fulfill all the commandments in obeying the first one first: love God and one another!

BREAKING BREAD

1 Corinthians 13, Matthew 5, Matthew 19:21

CONFIDANTS – COMRADES - CONSTITUENTS

There are 3 types of people in our lives: confidants, comrades, and constituents. Confidants are persons with whom one shares a secret or private matter, trusting them not to repeat it to others. Trustworthy, loyal, and true, this one has no hidden agendas and are for you sincerely.

Comrades are companions who you can share your activities in a organization world, this one is a fellow, someone that is for the same cause as what you do, and they come together for that purpose, but they are not really for you. They are for what you are for. You can get along with them because you believe the same (like liberals together and conservatives gathering themselves).

Constituents are people who are call themselves Christians like you but you don't actually know them and you don't know if they believe the same as you. You see them all around because they follow and meet others Christians on social networks. They just read what you say but never like your post publicly even though they agreed. They read your books and post about it in secret but don't let anyone know that they have anything to do with you or agree, but in secret they admire you. I believe if we are a family of God, we all get to be confidants but because of religion and pride we have this.

Every single one us has been one of these to somebody! My goal is not to man please but to be a peacemaker. One is from religion; one is from the Kingdom of God. It's time for us to all be real with who and what we are. There is nothing hidden that God will not manifest with His light. It's time to not only be for what God is for but be there for one another. One is false love! One is true love!

OLD? NEW? OR HYBRID?
What are you?

God used an ex-Pharisee to bring the body of Christ into maturity and still is! On the road to Damascus, Paul was on a mission to destroy the testimony of Jesus, to burn, stone, and kill any witness with the power of God! So, what did almighty God do? He sent an encounter of the power of God to Paul. What the law could not show him, the Holy Spirit encountered his life, changing his mind, his heart, his direction, and even changed his name. Within a few days, it totally transformed a man of the law to a man of faith, grace, and truth. From a murderer to a man of love! What the law could not do in his life because the letter of the law produced death and condemnation!

There was no man able to keep or fulfill it but one man named Jesus Christ! So, Jesus encounters Paul and changes everything: his direction, his purpose, and his heart! Then He gives him a torch to finish the work that Jesus started! This man never walked one day in the flesh with our master and teacher but preached the Kingdom of God in righteousness, holiness, and truth, and got mysteries downloaded and wisdom from above! What the law could not do, the baptism of the Holy Spirit did. What the law could not do, Jesus did on the cross!

Then, we never saw Paul once pointing people back to the powerless law of the works of the flesh, but on the contrary, because even with all his knowledge, he continued to point people to holiness that the law could not produce, and to righteousness that the law could not produce. He spoke things by the Spirit that revealed Jesus all through the Word from the beginning to the present! That's what God wants from us with this treasure in our vessels! Law produced death; the cross produced life!

Here are some things that the law produced. The children of Israel, **Romans 10: 12**, had unbelief even after they saw with their own eyes the Red Sea parting, the rock springing water, quail and manna falling from heaven, miracles, signs, and wonders! They could never get their flesh under submission. The minute Moses went up the mountain to get instructions, they built idols out of gold and fornicated. The law only produced a system of accusation and death. It stoned Steven. It dragged a woman through dirt ready for judgment! We can go on all day. Finally, the law killed the only perfect man who walked on the earth. Jesus was our example of no matter how perfect you may be, the law will bring death. No matter how much you get things right on the outside, you're still filthy as a dirty rag!

So God sent His son in the form of a servant so we could perfect love and walk perfectly as He is. So by being born again from above, He would write on the tablets of our heart, not on stone!

God is now using His finger of deliverance, working in us to deliver us to become the sons of God! He would write on the tablets of our heart, not on stone! By grace, He is working in us that our faith may be perfected in love, working righteousness in our inward parts as we become one with the fulfillment of the law, Jesus! Now Paul, in **Romans chapter 13**, this man of the law when he was Saul, said what our Lord said and also confirmed what commandments Christ is talking about observing. In verse 10, it says love worked no ill toward his neighbor: Therefore, LOVE IS THE FULFILLMENT OF THE LAW.

So then, he said that it's time to awaken out of sleep: Now your salvation is nearer than we first believed! Then in **Romans chapter 14**, He talks about eating and drinking ordinances, not to judge people on what they eat and what they drink. In it, he says one believes he can eat all things; another who is weak eats herbs (vegetables). Then it says in the next chapter, let he who eats not despise the one who doesn't eat. Let not he who eats despise him who does or judge him that eats.

God receives him. Then he talks about one man esteems one day above another, and for another, every day is the same! Let every man be fully persuaded in His own mind! Then one regards it to the Lord and one regards it not to the Lord! Just thank God in all you do to the Lord, and you are in righteousness. It's all about the heart again! As long as you live and die for God, you are His!

Then in verse 13, he says do not judge one another, and let no one put a stumbling block in your brother's way! Then it says I know and am persuaded there is nothing unclean of itself, but if you say it's not clean, then to you it's not! FREEDOM! Then verse 17: The kingdom of God is not meat or drink but righteousness, peace, and joy in the Holy Spirit.

Come on! This is amazing. It will never be what you do on the outside that makes you righteous on the inside but what we allow done on the inside that changes everything on the outside and on our flesh. This is the only thing God accepts and approves: my faith in His power and my obedience to His Cross. By picking up my own, I am now a living sacrifice! Then it says meat does not destroy the work of God! But then Paul says don't throw it in their faces. Paul says he rather you be like them while with them if it causes them to stumble, so don't mock what others feel like doing if that helps them by doing it! It is all about God writing his commandments on our hearts! Then it says it does not matter what you eat unless you eat without faith. What you do without faith is sin! Wow, that is deep and so clear!

Now let's see what Paul is saying in Hebrews. The only way to get the full counsel of God is to eat the whole book and let it not depart out of your mouth! In **Hebrews chapter 7**, he talks about the priest of the old covenant! Then he says, **"Who was made, not after the law of a carnal commandment but after the power of an endless life!"** (verse 16)

He says next about a disannulling of the OLD then for the law to be made nothing perfect, but bringing a better hope, we draw near to God (verses 18-19). The law made men the high priest; in the new covenant, Jesus consecrated us forevermore! Next, he said now Jesus is the mediator of a better covenant that is established on better promises! It says if the first covenant was faultless, then no place should be sought for a second!

Then it said for the day will come that I will make a new covenant with the house of Israel and the house of Judah! In the new covenant, I will put laws in minds and write them in their hearts. I will be to them a God; they will be my people, just like when I took them by the hand and led them out of Egypt!!! The last verse says a new covenant is made, first the old has decayed, waxes old, and is ready to vanish away!! Amen!

Then in **Hebrews chapter 9,** the first covenant had ordinances of divine service and a worldly sanctuary and a tabernacle with all things element, but now we are the tabernacle of God, our PRAYER is incense, His candle is in us. LIGHT is in us! Bread is in us, the Word of God.

His GLORY is in us, the gold, the treasure! Now we are priests of our temple! The Ark of the Covenant is in those who are born again. The old stood by meats and drinks and divers washings and carnal ordinances opposed on them until the time of reformation! Christ being the High Priest is a greater more perfect tabernacle. If the other blood was working, how much more the Blood of Christ through the eternal spirit purges us from dead works of the flesh to serve the living God!

For this, we have the New Testament! Moses, according to the law, took the blood of calves and goats with water, scarlet wool, and hyssop, and sprinkled both books and the people, saying this is the blood of the testament that God enjoined unto you! So now we have the Holy Spirit of God living in us. As we crucify our flesh and as we submit to Him, the law of God is being written on our hearts and in our minds. They are being renewed by the perfection working in us to become sons of God!

The old covenant was works of the flesh on the outside. The new covenant is the work of the Spirit on the inside. Just as the tabernacle of old, we are the tabernacle of God, changing us from faith to faith, and from glory to glory. That is the hope in us! The same power that raised Christ from the dead dwells in us who are born again, so fulfill all the law by obeying God and all He commands you, and you will be perfect in love and truth!

Jesus said my words are Spirit. They are life. The Word tells us that those who are led by the Spirit of God are the sons of God, not those who are led by the flesh or the law. He also says that the Spirit will guide you into all truth. The Spirit of God in us does not make us lawless but on the contrary, godly. As we focus on Jesus, He is being put on us and in us. We, too, have the ability to fulfill all things. In Him, we are a new creation!

Paul put it like this:

"Knowing that a man is not justified by the works of the law, but by the faith of Jesus Christ, even we have believed in Jesus Christ, that we might be justified by the faith of Christ, and not by the works of the law: for by the works of the law shall no flesh be justified. But if, while we seek to be justified by Christ, we ourselves also are found sinners, is therefore Christ the minister of sin? God forbid. For if I build again the things which I destroyed, I make myself a transgressor. For I through the law am dead to the law, that I might live unto God. I am crucified with Christ: nevertheless I live; yet not I, but Christ liveth in me: and the life which I now live in the flesh I live by the faith of the Son of God, who loved me, and gave himself for me. I do not frustrate the grace of God: for if righteousness come by the law, then Christ is dead in vain." Galatians 2: 16-21

Jesus said I come with a new and better covenant so they will be mine and I will be their God. So, what was once producing death in me is now producing life in me. Let's have dove's eyes.

Be holy as He is. Let the power of the cross crucify all flesh so that the kingdom of God in you can take all dominion around you! In this, we have faith in that shed blood. We have this new covenant. We are the righteousness of Him. We are no longer of this world but pilgrims and ambassadors of where we came from. We marry the lamb. So let this mind be in you that is in Him, the author finisher of our faith! One God, one Spirit, in communion with the TRUTH.

{ When carnal board members and when the lust for titles try to set someone (or themselves) in the Church (Ephesians 4), this is what we get:

- Pastors cooking out with wolves

- Fishermen/evangelists drinking by the lake with sinners

- Teachers feeding students with leaven

- Prophets tickling ears

- Apostles building with no blueprint from heaven

- No perfecting of the saints

- No work of the ministry

- No edifying of the body of Christ

- No unity of the faith

- No knowledge of the Son of God

- No perfecting of the new man

- No reaching the measure stature of the fullness of Christ

Do you see it? What demonic damage.

Marlene Roessiger

**"They were continually devoting themselves
to the apostles' teaching and to fellowship,
to the breaking of bread and to prayer."**

Acts 2:42

EMPTY OR FULL

Everything God does in the scripture, I believe, has a purpose and a voice. For example, we see Jesus going to a wedding in the New Testament. His mother tells Him that they were out of wine. It was so prophetic. It was a sign that man was empty. The old was not working, and it was dead, empty. So, His mother looked at the servants and said, "Whatever He tells you, just do it!" Sometimes we need to just do it! In this prophetic act, God showed me that this was a sign of the infilling of the Spirit.

There were six empty water pots. Six is the number of man! Man, under the old covenant, was empty and full of hypocrisy and religion. They needed to be filled with living water. If you only knew what is in front of you, you would have asked for living water! This living water will clean the inside. Those pots were for the washing of the outside! He does not want to give you a little but wants to fill you to the top so that people can come and draw out of you God Himself!

So when they filled these pots with water, it turned into wine. This was a representation of the new covenant God would make with His people. The Torah in you! The glory in you! The living water in you! The new wine in you! The Old Testament speaks of sour grapes that they drank. This was a representation of the old covenant that is decayed. Without Jesus, all you can be is sour and miserable. Look at how many are still in bondage and blind. It also says, **"No man also having drunk old wine straightway desireth new: for he saith, The old is better." (Luke 5:39)** We have the same battle going on in the body even today! The Word is TRUE!

Then we see the head guy of the wedding, not knowing what was done, saying, "Usually you give the best wine first."

"When the governor of the feast had tasted the water that was made wine, and knew not whence it was: (but the servants which drew the water knew;) the governor of the feast called the bridegroom, And saith unto him, Every man at the beginning doth set forth good wine; and when men have well drunk, then that which is worse: but thou hast kept the good wine until now." John 2:9-10

This is a prophetic utterance about the New Covenant. God would make a better and perfect covenant as we become one with God, filled with God and His love and TRUTH.

A New Covenant, a new wine! This is good! He did not know where that came from. We don't know where the Spirit comes from. He may come from the South, East or West, but when it hits you, you know it is good. We know it comes from God. Jesus came from God. He sent Himself back on the Earth to fill all the people of God with Himself. His name is HOLY, so He makes us holy as we partner with our creator in submission and in obedience to Him as He is in us and He restores all things, even our soul.

Right after the wedding, Jesus did go to the temple, and He cleaned it out – so prophetic again. Now we are the temple. He is cleaning us all up, from the inside out! Jesus is the way. We have a better covenant right now. God is not only angry with the one that is selling but with the one that is buying lies, the religious books and CDs and the anointing. It was about the sacrifice. There was none. You better bring the sacrifice. Who is the sacrifice? You are! We become the temple of God.

Jesus said that He will destroy the temple and in three days He would raise it up. His zeal is for you and for me to be the temple of God made by Him. They always look in the natural. God is spirit. All shadows are being seen by those with the new wine.

Be filled with the living water and the water always will turn into wine: a new creation! Old things have passed away. All things become new. "All" means no more old but "all" becoming new.

God forbid the mixing of the blood of bulls and goats with the blood of Jesus, how dare you? If you mix a little bit, it is like you are mixing a lot! God ordained us to be the new covenant believers after the resurrection. Jesus is the living bread and the lamb of God. Period! Hebrew roots? I don't think so. Who was Jesus first, a son of David or a son of God? Where is Jesus sitting now? In Israel or on the right hand of God? Where are we from and where are we sitting? Time to come up higher into your inheritance in heavenly places. Time to grow up into the fullness!

The Holy Spirit wants to take us to the land of joy, peace, and righteousness! Pride, rejection, let's kill this all. The Holy Spirit is renewing our old thinking. There is no power in the old covenant except by prophets. That is why the Holy Spirit came! To give us power to be sons of God.

True Gospel: Live it! Know it! Be it! Demonstrate it! Manifest the Kingdom of God! This is the new wine in you! Cast out all religious dogma and division.

We need to hear the voice of the Father! People out there are waiting for the chance to stone you. They are the children of the devil! Hear the voice of the Father and nothing else matters. They are puffed up on themselves. They have no power. They are critical and judgmental. There was no freedom in the old covenant. Everyone was in bondage. If you are still in the old, you are still in bondage. Only who the Son sets free is free indeed. The Word says, "The old and new can't be mixed. They will both be sour." Try it. It's scientific. It also said that they said, "The old is good and enough."

"No man having drunk old wine straightway desireth new: for he saith, The old is better." Luke 5:39

But if it was good enough, then God would have not made a new covenant! He also said that you cannot put old wine in new bottles or wine skins. He has saved the best for last: the one new man filled with God. He says if we mix the new and old, we will sour it all. Mixture was always spoken about in the Torah. Don't mix seed. God had the new covenant planned before He ever made the old. The church was planned even before man was created!

We are His new sons and daughters! Jeremiah was just prophesying what God wanted to say, but he himself did not understand it. Now Paul did! Paul had an encounter with the Truth.

The dead love to worship the dead. We worship the one that died but is alive again!

There are types and shadows of Jesus all over the Old Testament. I love that! It is all about that! Seeing Jesus everywhere and what He did on the cross! We are married to the lamb of God! We need to be connected to Him. This is communion. If you don't understand what I am saying, you need to be born again! I don't blame you for not reading the Bible because your mind will never grasp it! The letter will kill you if you don't become born again.

I am not here to teach you anything but to keep you focused on the One that will teach you all things. Knowing Him is to know how to do it. Knowing Him is to know your purpose. You can gain everything else but lose Him! In the end, what will matter the most: Are you a good and faithful servant? Or are you a worker of iniquity? It does not matter what your calling is. Your calling does not matter anything, but this is what you need to worry about: at the end, which one will you be: a faithful worker full of faith in Him or a worker of iniquity?

When God gives you revelation about something, you will find confirmation everywhere, from Genesis to Revelation! You are called to be an epistle read by all men, written not with ink, but by the Spirit of God, not in tables of stones but in the fleshly table of your heart! Not that we can do anything in our strength, not by might, not by power, but by Him – the new wine! If all you know is God, you are an able minister! Not of the letter but of the Spirit. Just do it! You have the power to break the chains! Just do it. Just do what He says. He will set you apart. The power has to do with the Holy Spirit in you! Those who believe will do great things, not those who have a title, not those who keep ordinances, but those who obey Him that are led by the Spirit.

The ministration of death was written in the stones. We have so-called ministers who stand up in the platform glorifying themselves when the real ones can't even stand in His presence because of the weight of glory!

Exceeding glory! You are one of those pots that He wants to fill and turn into wine! In the beginning, God created us into the image of God. And Jesus comes. The Lord keeps changing us into the SAME IMAGE! Any part that lacks, He fills with His fullness. This is the new way: filling us with living water. He wants to crack you, break you, and pour you out! A broken vessel!

People thought that John the Baptist had a lot, but everyone that has this new wine is greater! We have the same as Jesus WITHOUT MEASURE! Do you understand it? Do you know the Word? Better yet, does the Word know you?

God wants to break us! He will shake everything that can be shaken so everything that will last is HIM! Get all He wants to give you. God, help us to know you and who we are in you! Our identity does not come from man, but from above! We need to be turned from the inside out. God, we want to know you more and more. Anything we go through is to produce oil in us! All the blasphemy, stones, and persecution will help us to keep what He has given us today. New wine in new bottles is the new covenant spoken by the prophet Jeremiah!

Let our eyes be opened, let our ears be opened, that we may all become sons and daughters of the living God, God residing inside the man He created. Out of you will flow rivers of living waters. Remove all the stumbling blocks. If you are empty by choice, repent. If you are full, get some more! It is His desire for all of us to be partakers of this great new covenant and to drink from the cup of this new wine! In the wedding supper of the lamb, only new wine is served in Christ! Enjoy it today! Remember some last words before the crucifixion, **Mark 14:24-25:"And he said unto them, This is my blood of the new testament, which is shed for many. Verily I say unto you, I will drink no more of the fruit of the vine, until that day that I drink it new in the kingdom of God."**

BREAKING BREAD
John 2, Luke 5:30, Jeremiah 31, Hebrews 8, 2 Corinthians 13

EITHER FOR HIM OR AGAINST HIM

Judas was not focused on Jesus. He was a thief. What thieves do is they take what does not belong to them. This is the most anti-love act, to steal one's sacrifices, one's possessions, what someone has labored for. It's one of the most selfish spirits. He betrayed Jesus because he was not led by the Spirit of God. He was led by the anti-Christ spirit. Mary did not care. All she wanted to do was to anoint this man and love on Him sincerely.

Jesus blew the Spirit of God on them at that time. Nobody could be born again until the baptism of the Spirit after the cross. The more you die to yourself and let that seed fall into the ground, the more you will be like Him. When the woman brought the oil, she was being led by the Spirit of God, not by religion, not by self-seeking motives like Judas with the religious spirit. She was anointing him for burial. God is anointing us for living burial. When you are dead, you rejoice with those that rejoice. There is joy when we die. Who was in unity with Jesus? Martha was busy. Judas was stirring the disciples up in indignation with jealousy and envy.

Only Mary was being led by the Spirit of God, unlearned, unselfish, and even unaware of the prophetic act. God took Judas out before he contaminated others in the apostolic move that was about to shake the earth. They had not understood about the body of Christ. They grew up around religion. Jesus went on and washed their feet. And Peter asked: "Who is the greatest in your kingdom?" Jesus said the one who is the servant of all, the least of these. I wash your feet; you wash their feet. I lay down my life; you lay down yours. Judas was not for Jesus. He was for what He thought Jesus was for, but when He found out that it wasn't what He wanted or believed, He went solo and went to the religious leaders' system and became anti-Christ just like them. He saw the power of God. He saw miracles. He saw passion. He saw the love. He saw the Truth but just could not see things the way Jesus did.

Jesus is not asking for your money but your heart, not your possessions but your heart. Jesus knew that Judas was the son of perdition, but He kept on loving him. The anointing comes through the death. It is the death of a man that brings anointing. Love has no rights. When we begin to love as He loves, then the kingdom is here. When we lose our life, we will have His. When we stop worrying about our fame or our greatness, He exalts us. So many say they were with Him, but when it came down, the heart of man will always be revealed. Those who stuck by Him became glory carriers. The religious and self-seeking ones committed spiritual suicide from Saul to Judas. God is testing hearts. Who will carry His Glory without touching what is God's?

We need to let God heal us so we can live a resurrected life. Jesus never sinned against His brothers, His disciples. Never sinned against them! Peter cut off the ear of the soldier, but Jesus protected them. Jesus put that back! "That's my Peter! I will cover him." Jesus will always put that ear back! We must guard our hearts! This was the first guy ever seen to commit assault and battery on a law enforcement officer and go home with no cuffs on! Come on! Jesus, because of the heart of Peter, not perfection or anything else, took his place, and Jesus is still taking our place today! As long as we are for Him and we are not against Him, but if we are against Him then what else is left? We must be one body, one accord, in one Spirit!

Love is patient = free. When you walk in love, you walk in freedom.

Jesus was focused on the one that was led by His Spirit. Let's focus on Him and His Spirit so He will continue to anoint us for burial! Make sure our kisses are in sincerity and in Truth!

BREAKING THE BREAD
John 12

This spirit that Jesus was rebuking in some people was the same spirit that was trying to point people to the law when the law was pointing to Him. This is what Jesus was trying to show them! This same spirit is masquerading as believers and followers of Jesus when they deny His Spirit and His Word, now only pointing back to the dead when He is alive. The blind cannot see and the deaf cannot hear what the Spirit is saying to the church now. They would rather follow Moses who was speaking of Jesus than follow Jesus now. The worst thing is they can't do it either without the Spirit. There are so many in bondage. The letter kills, but Jesus is alive. Follow Him in Holiness and in Truth. He is the WAY. He is not lawless and neither are you if you walk in the Spirit. You are in Christ. This is the New Testament of my blood. Drink it!

**"Verily, verily, I say unto you, Moses gave you
not that bread from heaven; but my Father giveth you
the true bread from heaven."**

John 6:32-35

THE ANTI-CHRIST SPIRIT AND KORAH

There are no new spirits, evil or holy under the sun. So Mary with the oil brought her sacrifice to Jesus, her gift for His body for burial. Judas did not like that at all. Korah was saying, "We all are the same." Judas was saying, "Look at Him, Guys, we all do the same." Korah says, "We are all holy. Why follow Moses?" He lifts himself up and so on (we know God set him in). These two spirits are the same: anti-Christ or anti-headship, anti-government of God, anti-anointing, saying we are all equal and we are, but not in the sense of Godly government. Judas gets ticked off from the religious spirit that motivated him in jealousy that was stirring others in indignation to also come against Jesus, just as Korah did to come against Moses. Now we have many in the system of religion saying, "Well, let's do it our way. We don't need the Holy Spirit. We don't need the power. Let's just motivate them and encourage," representing the religious spirit in the New Testament. Korah did the same in the Old Testament, saying we are all the same. Do away with this Moses. Who does he think he is? Judas betrayed Him to the system of religion. Judas found his tribe. Judas said, "This oil and gift should be used for the poor, not the body of Christ." He gave gifts unto men for the perfecting of the saints, apostles, prophets, and so on, God's gift to us. We have a religious system with puppet pastors not from God but man. The stone the builders rejected is being rejected now, an anti-Christ spirit with no power, no correction, no Godly leading. So the Bible said he was a thief and really cared nothing for the poor. That's like religion that raises money not to support God's government, not to support anointing, but to support the golden calf, to support themselves and dead works, paganism, and salaries for unanointed leaders, people running around with no vision, just a bunch of division.

Now Mary was anointing Him, being led fully by God's Spirit, blessing the body of Christ. Also, Moses in his office of administration was to help protect and lead the congregation, being led by God fire and the cloud and face to face. Now watch this. Korah wanted to take the gift that was Moses' away for the people were saying we don't need it, we can handle ourselves. We do it our own way (not God's way). We all are holy. Now in the New Testament they say we all hear God. We all are part of the body. We don't need God's government. This anti-Christ spirit in the church says we don't need to cast out devils, we don't need to correct people. God will do it. Just love them, pray for them. Judas also wanted to do it His way just like the religious system. We don't need Elijah. We hear God.

This spirit is anti-power, anti-Holy Spirit, and anti-God and moves in dead works. So, Judas wanted to steal the gift (oil) representing Holy Spirit which is the anointing. God set apart broken men and women, people He is using that He ordained, not man-ordained (like Matthias). They are to anoint the body of Christ, to bless and break yokes, the ones He anoints to help all of us to die to our fleshly desires and lust and prepares as a bride without spot and wrinkle. Only the humble will be washed and pressed. The rebellious will dwell in a system of man in a dry place.

Do all have oil? Hope so. Are we all anointed?

Let's see! We know it says that we all should be, but we all, if anointed, must pay attention not to be rebellious or the spirit of murder will rob the gift. We will never be as anointed as God desires if we don't follow His instructions. God gave these gifts to the Body for edification and raising up. So, it's the oil (Holy Spirit) in the gift (person) to the body that this spirit of religion is after. The anointing causes the Absalom spirit all over teaming with Jezebel to rob the people of the oil (gift) for their burial so they can all be raised to the same stature and measure of Christ. It is a spirit of murder and python choking out headship, cutting off John's head. This blew my mind when it was downloaded. Hope it blessed you.

{

If you believe in once saved always saved, then you believe once believed always believe. So where does the trying of your faith come in? Where is when Jesus said will I find faith on the earth when I come? A witness is a martyr. To lose your life now is to gain it forever. Either we are living as martyrs or dead ones. That's our portion. Work out our own salvation with Godly fear and honor. Those (martyrs) who will endure until the end shall be saved.

....

Blessed are the peacemakers, for they shall be called the children of God. Cursed are the man pleasers, for they are the children of the world.

SPIRIT OF CONFUSION

The spirit of confusion is on the prowl. When God is speaking, the spirit of pride will post a smokescreen post and will bring confusion to little sheep. Pride can't repent. It's not in their nature. It is so demonic and selfish! God told me to warn the people that if they do not humble themselves, He will! Social media is not the congregation of the righteous (or church). "They are My sheep," says the Lord. "If you hurt one of my little ones, it is better that you have a millstone tied around your neck and be tossed in the sea!" God always confirms His Word by two or three witnesses!

So here it is in the book of Jude, confirmation, all words from the throne!

"Likewise also these filthy dreamers defile the flesh, despise dominion, and speak evil of dignities. Yet Michael the archangel, when contending with the devil he disputed about the body of Moses, durst not bring against him a railing accusation, but said, The Lord rebuke thee. But these speak evil of those things which they know not: but what they know naturally, as brute beasts, in those things they corrupt themselves. Woe unto them! for they have gone in the way of Cain, and ran greedily after the error of Balaam for reward, and

perished in the gainsaying of Core (Korah). **These are spots in your feasts of charity, when they feast with you, feeding themselves without fear: clouds they are without water, carried about of winds; trees whose fruit withereth, without fruit, twice dead, plucked up by the roots; Raging waves of the sea, foaming out their own shame; wandering stars, to whom is reserved the blackness of darkness forever." Jude 8-13**

This is Jude speaking to New Testament believers!

Once saved always saved? - Not according to GOD. I have roots in love (Christ), and God never changes. I can lose my salvation if I don't endure until the end. I suggest that you read the entire book because your pastor most likely won't!

DEFINITION: *dignity*

1. *the state or quality of being worthy of honor or respect:*

    "a man of dignity and unbending principle"

synonyms: stateliness, nobility, majesty, legality, courtliness, augustness, loftiness, lordliness, grandeur, solemnity, gravity, gravitas, formality, decorum, propriety, sedateness

2. *a high or honorable rank or position*

So, God keeps watching you. He sees all the spots. God said He will have a bride in one accord without spot or wrinkle.

The spots are being exposed. They are mavericks coming against:

- God's Word
- God's authority
- God's anointing
- God's children walking in truth
- God's ways

God is sifting. He is dividing. He is leading!

Facebook has slowly taken the fear of the Lord from so many. Satan is planting false leaders and teachers, confusing children of God, making them prideful then blowing out their light. We are in a revolution of humility. Without it, you will not be covered. Without the fear of the Lord, you will be made dumb and blind!

The thief comes to steal, kill, and deceive, but He can only do it to the children of pride! Time for not exalting ourselves above God! Get in our inherited position to receive the full blessing of God!

Keep your eyes open. It's a shame that many who are naked are being revealed only to those who are clothed! CAN YOU SEE IT! If you can't, it's time to get some clothes on because everyone sees who is walking in the full counsel of God!

MORE DEEP THOUGHTS

God has been speaking to me for the last two days. God showed that so many have given themselves a pulpit on Facebook, building their own following. God also showed me that unless God builds anything, we labor in vain. He also said that many have been puffed up and very disrespectful in posts and toward God's ordained voices, with opinions and attacks. Then He said to write this: What if tomorrow your social media was taken down and you had no way to reach, teach, or share with people?

What has God built in your life? Will you have disciples? Do you have community with the body outside social media? Because God is doing tons of things. His Spirit is moving everywhere. Do you have strong relationships outside of Facebook? He has Glory in the house. He said that one day nakedness will be revealed. Many will be alone because they have forsaken so much because of their reliance on the beast. We will all be fleeing this mountain soon. Do you have a family besides the facade of a Facebook family? This is a plea from the throne of God. Find your tribe. The anti-Christ spirit and religion have made people mavericks in a sense by becoming media gods. Their identity is from Facebook! Step back! Think! If Facebook disappeared tomorrow, where would you be? Who would you be? How would you be? Most would be traumatized. Have we created such a soul tie with it? Are we building His kingdom? Are we building a following? Because Facebook has released a maverick spirit on so many talented and gifted saints. But so many say whatever they feel because they think that just because so many agree with them, they have a right but we are not of the world. It must be from God; if it is not, it will all disappear. I did meditate on this and was, "Wow, God." I thank God for my family and my community in one Spirit that God is building. Don't take this lightly. I hear His voice. Put our trust in Him.

There are Christians like you but you don't even know them or if they believe the same as you. You see them around because they follow and meet on Facebook. They just see what you say but never like your post even though they agreed. They read your books and post in private but don't let anyone know that they have anything to do with you or agree, but in secret they admire you. I believe if we are a family of God, we all get to be confidants but because of religion and pride we have this.

Every single one us has been one of these to somebody! My goal is not to man please but to be a peacemaker. One is from religion; one is from the Kingdom of God. It's time for us to all be real with who and what we are. There is nothing hidden that God will not manifest with His light. It's time to not only be for what God is for but be there for one another. One is false love! One is true love!

SOCIAL MEDIA

{ ATTENTION !!! Very concerned – I see many lonely women and men having a soul tie with social media. One minute they are blessing, and the next they are cursing. – So many of their battles come from attacking things that they have not been sent to attack, such as ministries that are in error. In one breath, they are releasing hope and love. Then they are cursing and bringing division. The problem is that Satan has gotten a hold of them from offense and rejection because they are being led by emotions, not the Holy Spirit. God has prophets to expose, overturn, and to uproot things, and they have the grace to do it. So these lone star Facebook prophets see and hear truth that bears witness in their spirit, and then they think they have the right to get on their megaphone of Facebook and be a prophet. Then they get attacked and tormented because God did not tell them to do what they are doing. So it's done in the spirit of truth, not in the Spirit and Truth, and this is what we are all to move in. So with them going in so many circles, taking a little truth here and there, they actually acquire friends. There are so many tribes, but they really don't belong to anyone but their own social media following that they call family who ends up thinking and acting just like them; not an ordained or organic church family, but people all over the nation that came in agreement with their belief system.

What ends up happening is cultish because they end up liking and standing for one another, not in pure truth, but in their wounded, safe place, seeking their daily affirmation from a social media fix, not seeing the wolves and the Jezebels that are luring them and all undercover agents of the enemy who end up attacking sheep with them out of wounds and offenses. This is major! It is happening on a global scale. God says enough!! Spewing out their opinions – some of their post comments are spot on; some are so off. Like criticizing one musician and honoring another when the other actually has more secular music and sin than the one they are dissing. Then in one hour speaking peace and unity and the next cursing and criticizing others with the same mouth: fresh water and salt water! When it all ends up in a bowl, it is gall and bitter!

Only those with clean hands and a pure heart shall see God. Not everyone is absolutely perfect, but those who are not sent are actually causing division and discord. Let God and the Word and the prophets do their job so you can stay in Papa's arms. What you need to do is repent and give yourself a break and enjoy the ride because the weight and the price is too heavy for your weak vessel to carry. Let those who are chosen do it. Let Elijah do what Elijah is called to do, and if you try to be an Elijah when you are not graced or anointed or called to that office, you will become Jezebel! Mark my words! I have seen this happen hundreds of times! I pray that all see this warning from God. If the shoe fits then repent. Walk in pure love.

"For we [being] many are one bread, [and] one body: for we are all partakers of that one bread."

1 Corinthians 10:17

WHAT IS TRUE?

So many are false. So many are real. But without humility, you will never see it. Where there is holy, there is profane. Where there is true, there are lies. Where there is truth, there is false. Where there is real, there is fake. Where there is counterfeit, there is authentic. Where there is the fear of the Lord, there is false grace, false love, and man-pleasing.

Man-pleasing and God-pleasing are two different kingdoms. Two different gods. One is from the Kingdom of God and the other is from yours or from the spirit of man!

So, it is impossible to please man who is carnal and please God who is eternal! You will despise one and cling to the other! The spirit of religion HATES brethren walking in truth because they are compromisers, so they get the spirit of Cain on them! The spirit of Cain hates brethren that choose God over man. They hate people who reverence God and the Word of God because they themselves are compromisers, so they don't get received and anointed.

False fruits have no salt because they use fruits to direct men to them! Real fruits get hated, killed, and persecuted. Religion hides themselves in false fruits like fig leaves but stands naked and are being revealed in this hour! The remnant have been chosen. Just because you hang around the remnant does not make you one of them. Remnant do not man please but God pleases only! Remnant do not live on the fence holding onto religion and pretending to be free. They eat the Word. They live the Word. They are blessed.

Any doctrine of man is another gospel! False fruit movements eventually turn into lasciviousness. They all are nice, but they are not of God. There is a way that seems right to a man, but in the end, it is death! Man-pleasing will turn grace into lasciviousness. It will not correct, will not stand for one position, but will bend with every wind.

Love is not moved by emotions. It is a fruit of the Spirit! Love must be righteous, led by the Spirit of God, or it is counterfeit. Religion has a bunch of counterfeit fruit! These man-pleasers are cursed children because man-pleasing is a spirit of self. They are nice to everyone, but they are not salt.

Being all things to all men is not being like them as many come to falsely confirm nor is it sinning with them! Becoming all things to all men does not mean becoming a chameleon. Jesus hung out with the sinners, but He never sinned or approved sin. People don't take the full counsel. How can Paul become a Jew if later on, he said there is no Greek or Jew. He is born again, a citizen of heaven? Paul came to them in a position that they could understand him. So, he brings the pure gospel so they could understand. He still got stoned but not for man-pleasing but God-pleasing.

People use their social media as their pulpit. Everybody is right. Everybody is hearing God when they are not. Everybody is saying, "Thus saith the Lord," when He has not said anything to them. Maybe God Himself will shut down social media so the nonsense preaching will stop. There are so many making themselves Facebook pastors and flock followers because all are agreeing on what they like. They all like the same cherries that are being picked. I am doing spiritual warfare. We have to eat the whole tree!

Paul did not get his gospel from man or from himself but from God. If you don't know the Truth when the Truth was spoken, you are in a very bad place. God has somebody out there preaching the Truth! If everybody is wrong, God is wrong. When you come against the government of God, you are coming against God Himself! I tell you this: Everyone is not wrong and there is Truth in the land, not private interpretations. God does have people ordained to speak for Him. Then you have people speaking for God but are not sent. It is in the book of Jeremiah. They ran but I did not send them. **Jeremiah 23:21: "I have not sent these prophets, yet they ran: I have not spoken to them, yet they prophesied."**

Love corrects His children. Or you are a bastard. Maybe the anti-Christ and the false apostles are working hand and hand and nobody knows! Seers see, but you say don't show us. This promotes confusion. They call themselves apostles, but they are liars because they are man-pleasers.

God-pleasers are zealous of His presence! Of His truth! Of people that are lost. Of whom God is zealous for. The zeal of the Lord shall consume us all! The fear of the Lord keeps us. There is too much religious "manology" being mixed in the Truth. How many have set themselves up?

How about the ones that said: My words are from God when they are not? Do we have enough discernment? If you don't, you will be joining them without knowing. God does not tickle ears. He cuts off man-pleasing and fleshy-motivated word with the sword of the spirit. He cuts them off and gives you ears to hear.

These false leaders will find baby, born again believers and make religious man-pleasers like themselves. Liars, hearing not from the Holy Spirit, not moving in power, not sent by God but popular among the man-pleasers. Spiritual warfare sometimes is just a matter of turning them over. God is about to move on, but many will be stuck.

God's sword will knock the sword of man out of their hands. Anyone that has not salt in themselves can't have peace with one another. We are the salt, and we are supposed to enhance anything we touch, but if you are man-pleaser, you cannot enhance anything but your own agenda. You have not salt in yourself. What difference do you make? Is your agenda to be loved by all men? Are you ready to be hated by all men? God-pleaser is the only one ordained.

Make us true conduits of Truth. Iron sharpens iron. Anything else will dull our swords. Father, help us to not be offended. We break all unclean words, anything that is not of you, any chatter that is polluted. Guide us into all Truth. Your Word is Truth! We will not look at their faces. We will speak without looking at their faces. Clothe us and reveal us to ourselves that we may be clothed in your righteousness! Ground us in your Truth. Ground us in true love. A man-pleaser can never get a hold of what is true because it costs everything, and everyone wants a cheap gospel. But treasure is not cheap. It is glorious. Deep calls!

BREAKING BREAD

2 Peter 2, Galatians 1:6-15, Mark 9:34-50, Jeremiah 23:21

{

GRACE – LOVE – OUR WILL

The Grace of God is the power to become a son of God! Grace transforms us into the likeness of Christ! Grace is harder to live by and has more expected of you than the law. In the law, you had rights in perfect obedience. In Grace and the New Testament, you have no rights. You have been purchased. You are not yours anymore! Love your enemies and bless your haters. The false grace teachers don't even have a clue. God is raising up true Grace preachers that preach the Cross. Grace has everything to do with Him and a covenant paid for by BLOOD!

Love never relents. Love suffers long and rejoices in the TRUTH. If love sees sheep going astray, it will run after those sheep with endurance! Love does not ignore. It does not have pleasure in unrighteousness. Love sees good in all. Love is not silent! Love is bold. Love is full of zeal! Love is not a smile. Love is not a kind word. It's not a pat on the back. It's not a smile or a hug with hidden motives! Love will wrestle but will never take advantage. Love is pure. Love will see God! Love is God, and love never gives up.

God is showing me how strong man's will is. This is where religions get power from and empower religious spirits. That is actually a lying spirit. I need to say that because those with a religious spirit will say it's not in the Bible. God told me that if someone is determined in their heart and sets their mind to something, it's almost impossible for it to be changed, even if it is so clear in the Word and scriptures. Look at the scribes and Pharisees: How much clearer could it get when the Word came alive right in front of them? No matter what Jesus said they were stuck! Yes, they were blinded, but when Jesus came, He was ready to open their eyes. Some did repent. Most could not see revelation because of blind pride. Even with signs and wonders they still rejected Jesus. We still have this anti-Christ spirit in the church. Strong will empowers religious devils. Jesus help us! Not my will but yours! Let's keep seeing! TRUTH, GRACE, AND MERCY! Anyone that exalts themselves above the Word and the Spirit is a recipe for deception. God resists the proud and gives grace and revelation to the humble.

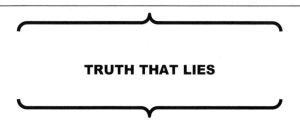

TRUTH THAT LIES

People have been sending me videos of so-called prophets from all over the world, some with millions of followers. It makes me nauseous because all it is is a show. All they do is prophesy. Do you realize how accurate fortune tellers are and palm readers are? Do you realize if you can learn to hear from God (Holy Spirit), you can learn to hear from the devil (unclean spirits)? When some claim words of knowledge come from God, and it's from the devil, it's called divination. Do you know that the devil and all his army know your entire past, every relative you ever had? Do know He knows more about you and your life, even more than you, especially if you are following Jesus, because we are told not to look back? Do you know that just because someone says something that is true does not mean it comes from the Spirit of TRUTH. Remember the woman with the spirit of divination? For three days she was saying the truth, but it was not from the Holy Spirit.

Real prophets get stoned in the so-called church while these ravishing wolves become idols. Real prophets preach the Word of God line upon line. These soothsayers barely ever open the Bible. Soothsayers put on a show to get everyone entertained and lift themselves up on how accurate they are. Real prophets point out sin in the church and sin in the lives of those who are in the fold. False prophets dance around and ignore sin and boast on how anointed you will be. They tell you every secret ambition and idol of your heart and give a holy interpretation to make you believe you can be worldly so God will use you in your will not His. False prophets and soothsayers are always pointing you to their gift, not to Jesus, pointing you to how accurate they are and always having to prove they are from God. Gifts don't set you free The Word in POWER transforms us and changes us from faith to faith and Glory to Glory.

> ➢ Real prophets point you straight to the cross, straight to Jesus and the Holy Spirit. They actually cast out demons and don't entertain people with demons.
> ➢ Real prophets are about God's business.
> ➢ False prophets are about show business.
> ➢ Real prophets point to the cross.
> ➢ False prophets point to gifts and manifestations, taking the glory.

I have news for all of them: Elijah is here! He is going to put a show on, one show: He is going to expose all the prophets of Baal. He is going to lead the remnant into Daddy's arms. All of them that love the wages of Balaam and hold these doctrines, unless they repent, will also be removed. Time is short. Judgment has been released on all those that love eating at those tables. Repent for the kingdom of God is here.

WOLVES

Wolves are very sneaky. That's why Jesus said they are in sheep's clothing. They mingle with an agenda. They try to isolate one or two sheep at a time. They don't come through the front door. (In other words, the Bible says the porter is at the door, meaning ordained seers for that pack of sheep; so wolves, hirelings, come in through the back door or side window.) So they prophesy in private, in parking lots, bathrooms, on messenger, and on social media. The devil has them deceived, thinking they are right, but they are always struggling to fit in, to communicate, and to fellowship on a pure level. Because of all the rejection, they operate in false love, that is, with false fruits. That is their biggest weapon. They say things, but what they say is full of confusion because if they said exactly what they meant, their agenda and cover would be blown. They study the sheep, wait for the vulnerable, and wait for an opportunity to steal the truth away. The youngest and the most on fire, hungry ones are its prey. But real anointing can peg them in seconds. That is why they operate sneakily and climb up in other ways.

The Bible says to prophesy openly and in front of all so all can judge. Wolves bring confusion. God is not the author of confusion. Leviathan is! He twists things to sound like one thing but means another. By words, they manipulate and deceive! Most wolves were sheep at one time, but jealousy and rebellion to God and authority made them a scatterer and not a gatherer. They promise you freedom while they feast with you, but inside they are ravishing! Beware of them crawling all over Facebook, camouflaging as missionaries, pastors, and sent ones, but they sent themselves. God is showing me that there are so many around us — unsubmissive mavericks of rebellion. The curse of rebellion is homelessness. Saints, do not forsake the assembling together, because if you do, there are wolves ready to steal and rob your food and your destiny. The steps of the Lord are ordered unless you walk solo. He never leaves you, so don't leave Him.

"This is the bread which cometh down from heaven,

that a man may eat thereof, and not die."

John 6:50

SPIRIT OF BALAAM & NICOLAITANS

"Who really wants the real Jesus (truth)?" I know just a few. Hope it's you!

As you read this, you will see that the spirit of Balaam works hand and hand with the Nicolaitans. But first, we need to study the heart of Balaam to understand the spirit of it!

So we are already seated with Christ in heavenly places. Beware of men who try to say, "They are taking people up to the heavens!" Beware of the doctrines of Balaam. Beware of doctrines that come from man and strange fire! He taught Balak to cast a stumbling block before the children of Israel! Jesus says that the same spirit is here in the end times as it was in the beginning times according to the book of Revelation! What did Balak want Balaam to do? To curse the blessed, to use him to come against God's elect, and to try to curse what God has blessed. Balak represents the enemy in our ears and the path of those who prophesy and preach not the cross and separation. He is using seduction.

"But I have a few things against thee, because thou hast there them that hold the doctrine of Balaam, who taught Balac to cast a stumblingblock before the children of Israel, to eat things sacrificed unto idols, and to commit fornication. So hast thou also them that hold the doctrine of the Nicolaitanes, which thing I hate. Repent; or else I will come unto thee

quickly, and will fight against them with the sword of my mouth." Revelation 2: 14-16

Balak was king of the Moabites. If Satan can get you, the blessed, to curse the blessed, you can become like Cain. In this message, we will focus on the heart of the blessed and also on how the blessed can become cursed with the curse if you allow your heart to become hardened or tempted to come against the ways of God.

The works of the Nicolaitans, doctrines, and the ways of Balaam are prevalent in the system we call charismatic or denominational clergy or the hierarchy pastoral church, the order of Constantine. The works of the Nicolaitans is a clergy setting and paganism mixed with the called out, holy, and set apart Gospel. They are run like the world! Worldly focused!

Balaam was the prophet of God who compromised and fellowshipped with the enemy of Israel. We see him now as the devil!!! He was being manipulated to curse. When we start to be tempted or to move in the flesh and become like the world, we will begin to act just like them and sooner or later get deceived like them.

Nicolaitans and Balaam work hand and hand! You see that if he could curse, he would curse, but HE COULD NOT CURSE WHAT GOD HAD BLESSED. If he could, he would have sold out. Balak tempted Balaam with fame, riches, and much honor from man, like some Christian TV, but God kept on blessing Israel. As long as Israel did well in God's sight, no one could touch them.

Balaam became a prophet for hire. So it is with the works of the Nicolaitans. It's a system for hire, a system of religious clergy and hierarchy run like the business in the World. Not Body ministry where every joint supplies to the Body of Christ moving in the Spirit, but it is a gift to show man. I would say itinerant prostitution looking for work and not advancing God's kingdom but advancing their own wallet.

Prophets for hire are all over the place. It works fluently in the denominations and in the system of the Nicolaitans, what we call organized religion. It is not apostolic but is pastoral clubs helping the needy, doing works of justice with no power. God brings these together because, in Revelation, the church of Pergamum worked hand and hand with the works of the Nicolaitans. You need a system to promote or pimp your prostitution. It is not heavenly-ordained but man-made, run by hired employees, not by God-ordained gifts, running in power just as a form of God but absent from God. They hire people to grow churches. Their networks and church growth steps are all carnal.

The church is not a place where you get promoted because of your degrees and knowledge. We need to make sure that our foundation is sure and sound! What you let in your heart will contaminate your gift. So if you have an assembly in a city and run it like a business and not a body and a family, you are operating in the works of the Nicolaitans. God says He hates this work. That's pretty heavy to ignore! The world system produces the spirit of Balaam. The apostolic is God's system and structure where the fruits are more important than titles, where gifts edify the body and are not showcased, and where we freely receive and we freely give.

Balaam really wanted that money, fame, honor of man, and popularity but was not able to curse Israel, so he explained to the king how to get God's people cursed. All the king had to do was to make sure the Israelite's intermarried with other tribes (world), which is something they were not supposed to do, and then they would lose the favor of God on their lives. So, while he didn't curse them, he wanted to. He explained how to get the job done; like always, the lust of the flesh. Satan uses temptation. When we eat it, it brings compromise. This is why the cross needs to be the focus.

We are not a business. We are a body ministry. All have access to God. All are priests and kings! This prophet went to the mountain of Baal and made sacrifices with the enemy. Prophets of God who are turning into prophets of Baal, they are all around us. The enemy tempts you to do what you are not supposed to do. You become a worker of iniquity. If you curse your brother, you become sons of iniquity. Because of compromise to fame and fortune, God's prophets are becoming prophets of Baal and teachers of Baal. If we seduce and use a gift to make gain, we will become just like Cain.

Balaam could not curse Israel so he found a way to put them under a curse. He tried to get them fornicating with the heathen. Mixture! When you stop fearing the Lord, you start cursing your brothers and sisters. He was supposed to be God's man, but he became a double agent, working with the enemy because of greed in his heart. He wanted to sell books and CDs for profit (NOW) and to be on Christian TV for personal gain. That's how he rolls today, bringing mixture of the world into the sanctuary of our hearts; prosperity prostitutes running church to church, venue to venue, for offering and gain, under the covering of 5013c pastoral Babylonian settings, being pimped by Nicolaitan foundations, false apostolic networks, always offering the next new revelation or program or impartation and selling their personal encounter. The only thing we need is the Word in power with the Holy Spirit. In their hearts, they say, "If I can get on Sid Roth, my ministry will take off." Works of the Nicolaitans is married to paganism. Selling the anointing does not affect them. Then they lose it.

Israel fell by the lust of the flesh. It married the things of the World. You yoke up with unbelievers. One sure sign of a Nicolaitan preacher is mixing paganism and the calendars of the world in with their messages, like Valentine's Day, Christmas, and Easter. None of these are in the Bible, so why would you use them in preaching or honor them in the assembly? Selling a prophetic book and selling a prophecy, is there any difference? Only in our Nicolaitan (GREEK) mindset, but that's why God is renewing His bride, giving us the mind of Christ.

We are not a business. We are a Body ministry. Stay under the blessings of God, and don't fornicate with any things of the World. Stay in line with the Word of God. Stay in Him! Whatever comes in must be holy and sound. The remnant will be attacked; many will try and curse it; stay holy and set apart.

Nobody in his right mind does not want money. If you don't, you are religious. If you don't, you missed a few things in the Word. You need money to advance the Kingdom. It's the love of it that we need to be delivered from. Love of the world is the root of all compromise.

Market place ministry is operating in the spirit of Balaam. Deep down it is all about money. We are already seated in heavenly places. We already have dominion over all the kingdoms of this world. God has given us back garden dominion and authority. We need to learn how to use it!

You want the blessings? Pick up your cross. If you pick up your cross, you will deny yourself. If you deny yourself, you will love your brother. If you love your brother, you will do well. There is plenty of scripture about who is from God and who is not.

Is the reason why you publish books because the last one made tons of money? Here is another tactic of Balaam: "Let me give you a chapter then you buy the rest." Is it not because you want to set the captive free? Is it not because you want to edify the Bride? Is it not because you want to reach many with the Truth? So your motivation is all wrong! You are merchandising God's people. Then you have gone the way of Balaam and are not an asset but a stumbling block. The cross is the only access to God and prosperity.

"Woe unto them! for they have gone in the way of Cain, and ran greedily after the error of Balaam for reward, and perished in the gainsaying of Core." Jude 11

The Lord knows how to deliver the Godly out of temptation. All of us are being tested by fire, even many in temptation around us. But if your heart is pure, if you are not following the corrupt desire of the flesh and not despising authority, if you are not presumptuous or self-willed, He will know exactly what to do to get you out of temptation. God has apostolic order on the earth. God's government does not get permission from the governments of the world, neither begs for handouts. God's government is the head and not the tail.

Don't forget the right way, the narrow way, and don't follow the way of Balaam. What is the way of Balaam? – Running with greed, great swelling words of vanity, soothsaying, ear-tickling, and compromised messages absent from holiness.

Outside of Christ is deception. This world is condemned. Stay in Christ, casting out the rudiments of the world. Be loyal to God and His holy Word. Keep speaking what He tells you to speak only. Do you think that outside of Christ you are stronger than the devil? Be loyal to His Word. Be loyal to His love. Keep on speaking whatever He tells you. Keep on loving whoever comes against what you are speaking. Keep loving and blessing whoever comes against you and what you are speaking. Bless and curse not;

repent often; check your heart daily. Let your meat be to do the will of the Father, the creator of all things.

BREAKING BREAD

Numbers 22:5-7, Numbers 22:11-12, Numbers 22:15-18, Numbers 22:41, Numbers 23:11-12, Numbers 24:10, 2 Peter 2, Jude 4-20, Revelation 2:12-17, Luke 6:26-40, 1 John 3

One thing that irritates the Holy Spirit is this: When God is exposing darkness and deceived wolves, the religious spirit will always say, "Well, pray for them." If prayer saved people, we would all be saved. If prayer made bad people good, we wouldn't need the power of the Gospel. Stop the high spirituality redirect. Preach the Gospel with all boldness! You can go in your closet, fast and pray for a year for Beyonce or Madonna and whoever else hates the Truth and loves iniquity, but until one "repents," until people fear God...and we will always have evil and always have reprobates. Do what the Bible says: PREACH THE GOSPEL.

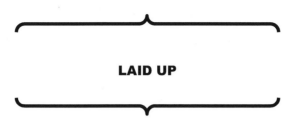

LAID UP

Let us soak up the full counsel of God. God is not double minded. He is the same yesterday, today and forever. Joseph brings a shadow of Jesus. God used one man to save a nation. Then One Man to save the World. The beginning always reflects the end. From the pit to the palace, from the jail to the throne...God is always Jehovah Jireh to His people.

There was already a famine for two years. There was corn in Egypt, and who was running the storehouse: Joseph! Who gave the dream to Joseph? God! Who stored up? Egypt. Not Israel. Who did God provide for with no toil? Who actually did all the work for preparing for the famine? Who has the promises of God? Is your name Jehovah Jireh? Or is His name Jehovah Jireh?

We have to learn that God provides all our needs. God used one man, one person, to sustain the whole nation. No matter what, God is watching a movie that He already made. He knows every part. When we walk in obedience and in Truth, He takes care of us.

So who is Jehovah Jireh? God. Abraham was tested. So many are failing the test. Some so-called prophets are even selling stuff for survival. Without faith, you cannot please Him. Don't follow any winds of doctrine to toss you or to make you fear. Any theory that comes against the writings of Jesus is not from God. We need to smash every man-made wisdom and teaching.

How can I have faith in my own kingdom and in my own strength? How can I build His kingdom when I am building my own kingdom? You will become anti-kingdom. Only one kingdom will stand. The wealth of the wicked shall be laid up for the righteous. If there is no food, He would even take your hunger away or send you angels to feed you. Even ravens. God is God in every season, in every minute in all time. These merchandisers must be stopped subverting whole houses.

What are we supposed to be doing every day? Building the kingdom within us. You can't take care of yourself and take care of His kingdom. First: His kingdom always! God will feed a whole nation using one man. God feeds His church with One Holy Spirit.

Joseph is the representation of Christ. It was not about Joseph. It was about God's purpose for that nation. What Joseph went through saved the whole nation. What Jesus went through saved us all! God is only pleased by faith. What kind of relationship is this when the Father is rich but the sons are broke? What did Isaac do in time of famine? Did he store up or did he sow?

Beware of the leaven of hypocrisy. God is your supplier or He is not. Don't pretend He is when you really don't believe. We made everything our god. They say one thing but they do another. If I preach Jesus, I better be eating from what I preached or I am a hypocrite! God is God or I better help Him.

Fear only God, not the economy, not the stock market. The very hair that is on your head, He knows it. God knows everything. He is testing your faith. Does the Bible lie or does it not?

We will have enough wisdom, and we won't strive to get anything. Those who strive are rebellious children because strife comes out of rebellion and fear, bringing toil every single time as it shows in the Bible. When we don't trust Him, we deny Him. He said: Take the land! But people are looking at the land, at the obstacles, and at the giants and are not obeying. We either see how big God is or we see how big the problem is.

Faith has a plus. Fear has a minus. It takes everything away: your joy, peace, favor. If you confess God, He will confess you. He cannot deny Himself: "When they bring you, when they persecute you, when they come to get you..." This sounds like the end times, but He will teach you what to say, what to do, and where to go. This is what He is building in you: a strong foundation!

Either the gospel is the gospel or it is not the gospel. False teachers, wolves in sheep's clothes, are bringing this demonic doctrine! People are giving power to the beast through the fear that the beast puts on them. Store up! Give me a break.

God will have a raven's delivery service to the remnant. Come on, Elijah, wake up! Perilous times will come. The Word talks about that, but this is why we have God. Sometimes God will tell you to keep something now because you are supposed to give later, not because of fear but for a purpose. He said, "Do not lay up your riches on Earth."

The churches are trying to be a friend of the World and keep their rights. The Constitution will be burned away and what are you going to do? The government of this World will turn on you and whatever you have will be taken anyway unless you take the mark. How foolish to become a friend of the World!

A man's life does not consist of the abundance of possessions. In the wilderness, there were no survival techniques – just follow the glory cloud by day and the fire by night. Expand His kingdom. If you are suffering, it is not because of Him but because you are disobeying. We do not trust in horses, chariots, and in the government but in the Lord - Jehova Jireh.

There is no American dream in the Kingdom of God because the American dream is all about you and comes with a lot of strife. What is the kingdom of God: joy, peace, and righteousness in the Holy Spirit! To be in the Holy Spirit, you must come out of the spirit of this age!

You laid up your treasure for yourself, but you are not rich towards God. Consider the ravens and birds: they neither sow nor reap. Daddy takes care of them. You will be persecuted for all the blessings. You will suffer because of it. He is training us to be good stewards of what He put in our hands. You can't add one cubit to anything anyhow.

How long is the famine? Do you know? How long will it last? Consider the lilies. Five barns, two barns, how much will be needed? Eventually, we will all need God. Start today. Put your trust in Him, not in your own strength.

Anything that comes against the gospel of Jesus Christ is the enemy of the cross, the enemy of faith, and anti-Christ. He wants to give us the kingdom, but He is taking the need for things out of us. All of our needs shall be added if you seek Him first.

If your treasure is in the kingdom of God, your heart will be in it. Always seeking the kingdom and His righteousness! There is no way to advance the kingdom of God unless the kingdom of God advances in you. He is not going to come when you think He is coming, but when you think He will not. Stick to the Word of God and be ready. The miracle does not happen with the digging or with the toiling. The miracle happens supernaturally by resting in faith. The Gospel is not a formula. It has rebuke, edification, and power. Faith is the only Gospel we should follow. Not fear.

What have you been laying up? The Word in **1 Timothy 6:19-21** tells us to lay up for ourselves a firm foundation against the time to come that we may lay hold of eternal life! Lay your treasure in the kingdom of God. This is the kingdom of faith. Seek first God. Seek Him always. He promises to be there for you whatever you go through. He knows! Let us walk in Spirit, not in doctrines of man and false prophets that lie to you and teach you to save yourself! There is only one strong tower, and it is not you. There is only one storehouse that lasts forever, and it is in heaven. Store up where there is guaranteed return, where you won't be stripped by the anti-Christ spirit.

BREAKING BREAD

Genesis 42, 1 Corinthians 3:1-3, Luke 12:43, Matthew 6, 1 Timothy 6:19-21

 ## WILDERNESS

God is prosperity but in the wilderness was a place to train them to trust in Him, not in their own strength or self or in the world (horses and chariots). The wilderness was a place to deliver them from want and greed and fear, not that God wanted them not to have, but not to COVET and to TRUST. HE IS MORE THAN ENOUGH (El Shaddai). Because the Promised Land was full of excess, that was the promise. So, when He delivered them, they were heading to the land of milk and honey, but God had to get Egypt out of them first! Why was His name El Shaddai? Because that came after Jehovah Jireh, the Provider. Jesus became poor that we might be rich. Also, prosperity is God...it's not a gospel! When He said you cannot serve two masters, He was speaking of idolatry. There was no way to love God with all your heart and love mammon. What you love you serve. Where your treasure is so is your heart.

So the problem with the PROSPERITY GOSPEL ISN'T PROSPERITY! It's their gospel and its motives, and the only Gospel is the Cross. The spirit of religion will rebuke you for wasting oil (precious treasure or costly perfume) and tell you what you should do with your treasures, but the (Holy) Spirit that gives will direct you. Religious spirits use logos to judge others. Those in the Spirit use logos to get you in the Spirit. Those who are led by the Spirit will be prosperous and have lack of nothing because God cannot deny Himself. Seek first His kingdom and His righteousness and all things He will add to you. The Bible says God rejoices in the prosperity of His children. Let us never seek His hand but His will. Know the difference in having and hoarding.

"Or what man is there of you, whom if his son ask bread, will he give him a stone?"

Matthew 7:9

EXPECTING GOD

If we are not in a posture of expectation, we are on the edge of becoming ritualistic. Whatever we do, we should expect Him. Expect Him in everything we do. If you lose expectation, you will start doing everything in His name but religiously. Without expectancy, you will become ritualistic.

Then we become complacent and apathetic. Every single minute of our lives we need to see Him, believing He will show up. We need to have a testimony on our lips daily. When we expect Him, He always shows up. This is how we are to live, like this normally.

Expectation brings desperation.

If you know that He is a rewarder, you will expect something from Him. God always happens. We are the ones that always stop happening. Then we think God stops moving, but He is not a man that He should lie. Could it be that we stop moving towards God?

We need to keep going after God diligently. That is desperation. His reward is HIM!

You may be doing something with a Godly form, but you are really denying its power if you don't expect Him. You can sing, go to the altar, do this, and do that, but you are never going anywhere because your hearts are not expecting anything.

They that come to God must believe that HE IS – a reward for those who seek Him – with persistence, without being weak, without giving up. Seek after Him hard, or you will begin to be dead.

We do things having a FORM OF GODLINESS but there is no power, no evidence, and no manifestation. Our hearts cannot deny His power.

I can't have faith for tomorrow. I have to have faith now because if tomorrow does not come, I will faint, but now is here, and it is for NOW. Or you become religious and lukewarm. We should not come together because we have to, but when we do things together, things happen because He is in the midst of two or three who are gathering in His name.

Compromise produces apathy which produces unbelief. Always expect something to happen! Expect Him to show up!

We are in transition right now for greater things. You should expect His reward every minute, every second, every day of every week.

Here is another thing that kills expectancy: It is familiarity! Jesus wanted to do mighty things in His city, but they did not believe. They thought, "He is just a carpenter." There was no expectation. He marveled at their unbelief. Then He left His town. Jesus healed a "few." It was not a good day for Him because He wanted to do so much more but no faith, no expectation. Start expecting, and you will see great things happening. People did not really believe. They were looking through their flesh. The kingdom of God is within you.

In **Mark 6:32-36**, there are people – sheep without a shepherd – expecting the great shepherd. The meeting happened right there because they were hungry. They got the best food of all. They all got lunch. They all saw a miracle. They were fed inside and out because they were following Him and diligently seeking Him. He fed them with two fish and five loaves. He fed thousands!

Some people hear a preaching without expectation, and nothing happens inside of them. Go back to that place of expectancy, and you will see what happens. Our reward is just Him! He looked to heaven! He expected Daddy to move! Jesus Himself expected something from His Daddy. Getting into the natural will stop you from receiving the supernatural.

Sometimes Jesus does great things but suddenly our hearts get hardened. Right after, Jesus went and rested after feeding thousands. Then their expectation ended. They did not consider what He did and let complacency take place. Then they feared for their lives and were toiling to get to the shore. Jesus came to walk on the water and could not believe that their hearts became hard so fast.

But others heard about Him who did not even know Him, and their expectation moved Him. The disciples should have expected more than anybody else, but people that were not even His disciples were hungrier than them. Let this not be us. Let us not get familiar in a way of losing our wonder!

We need to expect HIM, every day! Or we will come together, do this and do that, and get nothing. Our hearts full of unbelief will cause us to not expect any more. You need to peel off the flesh and see the kingdom of God inside of every one of us! Expect that kingdom inside your brother to manifest! When you stop expecting, you start living broken again. When we get old in our complacency, we need to be fixed on Him!

He wants us to be desperate for Him, every minute of every day, not just one day.

You have a name that sounds powerful, but there is nothing there. He wants to strengthen what is about to die. When we starting dying, we can't see right. We lose our senses. He is the God of the living not the dead, so expect Him to move because He is alive.

And if He is not moving, He is not dead, YOU ARE! Sometimes we know that He is in the house, but we don't seek Him. Come find Him! When your heart diligently seeks Him, you will find Him! You go and find Him! Get out of your place, go and find Him! He is here! He promised He is here! I will find Him! I will go and find Him! Sometimes we stand by the front door, and He is in the back of the room. You need to go and find Him. He is in the house because He cannot deny His Word.

He may come when you are not expecting, but you are not expecting anyway. When we come together we need to seek Him. People were thronging Him. They were pressing upon Him to touch Him! Sometimes your words, your actions, or your thoughts will push Him away because they are not full of faith. Be like the unbelievers that believed what they heard about Him. Even before they met Him, they were expecting from Him because of rumors they heard of Him.

It just takes two, in agreement, touching anything, it shall be done, if we are expecting. There has got to be faith in that agreement. Two or three in His name, He is there. If you are gathering just because and that is what we do, that is religion and just ritual. He is not there. When we gather expecting Him, He will not give us a stone or a scorpion. He is in the midst! He is in the midst! Be filled with expectation. I am not talking about works in the flesh but hunger in the Spirit!

Diligently seek Him full of expectation! The yearning! The longing! Going after Him! He always will reward you because of your faith. Faith is the evidence of your own expectation.

Let the dead bury the dead. We will not be complacent. We want Him every day of the week! Heaven is the limit. There is no limit with you. But don't listen to voices, or they will kill your expectation. Don't let religious chatter deceive you.

I believe that HE IS! He is I AM – not me – but HIM! Because He is! He is! He is! The gift of faith will come up in you like Samson! Strength to believe! Strength to seek Him, diligently! He will reward you because He is.

BREAKING BREAD

Mark 6:1-6, Matthew 13, Mark 6:32-36, Mark 3, Matthew 18, Hebrews 11:1-6, Revelation 3:1-6, 2 Timothy 3

{ God says you are amazing. You are fearfully and wonderfully made. The devil is a liar. No matter how many people tell you that won't matter until you believe God. Lies shut down even the best of them. Ask Elijah. Ask John the Baptist. We must believe the report of what God says, not what we think. It's not people. It's not places. It's you. You need to believe the Truth, and the Truth sets you free! You are amazing! There is one person you can never, ever run from. You will be with that person the rest of eternity. That person is you! Believe the Truth today. Your identity is not from what you think. It's from what He says. He is not a man that He should lie and you are a believer. Start believing and start loving you today.

YOU ARE THE GARDEN
IN THE KINGDOM

What we allow to be planted (words) are seeds. When we meditate on it, it is like watering it. It is going to grow. There is always seed time and harvest time. Seeds need time to grow. So God is giving us time to pluck any bad seeds out. Grace empowers you to pluck them out of your garden (heart). Some sow, some water. God gives the increase. Don't you think that in the devil's kingdom the same happens? The devil will give increase of the bad seed you did not pluck out, and that is the decrease in your life.

You need to pluck them out. Meditation on those seeds is like you watering those bad seeds. Whatever you enthrone on your heart becomes your god, your way, and your thinking. It is the weeds in your garden. Because only the Word of God is the good seed! Anything else is bad seed that will turn into weeds and thistles and prickers.

The Word of God says LET THIS MIND BE IN YOU (the mind of Christ). We don't wake up in bondage. We keep watering that bad thought so we think our way into it. That is weeds. Then it grows up and gets roots, and then it troubles our walk. The longer we keep it, the stronger it gets.

The kingdom of God is within you. The only way to change the World around you is to let the kingdom of God grow inside of you. But what you think, you will be! So check on what you meditate on!

God said we are the ground. Word can come to you in different forms, not only through your eyes, but through anything you hear. Sometimes the Word has not taken root in yourself. You need to meditate on that seed, not on what the devil tells you. You can't meditate on two things at once. It is impossible. You have two choices: to water the kingdom of darkness or to water the kingdom of light! Anything else is double-mindedness.

God gave us the mind of Christ. Anything that we hear differently to the Word of God, we need to dig that thing out and pluck it out! When you stop watering something, what will happen? It will die! Many will turn truth into lies because of bad meditation. You have to grab those seeds of life and water them. Keep on watering them! Make no provision for the liar. He is a liar and a thief! He will try to choke out every good seed.

The only seed that we should water is the Word of God. One day you water this one, another day you water the other one, you become an unstable man. You will receive nothing from God. You will be tossed to and fro. Water the seed of God! God gives the increase. Satan gives the decrease. Think on things above. Your mind is the filter to your heart. Reject what is not lovely, pure, truth, of good report, of praise, or just. Don't think on what is carnal but on the eternal. Meditate on what God says, not on anything that brings doubt. Whatever you eat that is not of God, you should spit it out. If your spiritual life is decreasing, you need to pluck out some seeds.

We must be a doer of the Word, not a hearer only. You are not deceiving your brother but yourself. When you are saying, "I can't do it," what you are watering is doubt and unbelief! Sometimes you are asking, "When will my mind get free?" When you get your thoughts/meditation on things above, when you meditate on the Word from above, on what God says.

If you meditate on what you really are, you will be. Unless you don't water that seed! Everybody wants supernatural things, but when you are walking with Him for a while, God is expecting you to do what you are supposed to. Do it. Water it. Meditate on it.

A disciple means to be a disciplined learner! A follower of the Word! I don't want to encourage you only. I want to see you change. As you change, you will encourage others because of His power that is in you changing you. It will give hope to others and glory to God.

I need to read it, drink it, and eat it. You can keep watering your mistakes, and that will get you in condemnation. It's your own fault. God does not water the mistakes we made, we do! The Bible says, "SPEAK IT." There is a place in God when you groan, and He understands it. Even that you do in faith. That groaning is your heart song unto Him.

He is not waiting for you to be perfect! Take your eyes off you. And He gives us authority to stay free once we are free. Keep your eyes on Him. He is the Word.

If not, we will be up and down. Increase and decrease! You need to go from faith to faith. If you go from faith to fear, you are watering that evil seed! That negative satanic seed can cause you to be mad at the Word. Its plan is to choke out of you the good seeds and beautiful fruit! Don't let that happen! Satan comes to steal God's Word, to kill your growth, and to destroy your increase. So many of us get so mad at God that we keep running away from Him! We all love to run when it is time for correction, but that correction will keep us alive!

Guard your heart! Salvation is in enduring until the end. Endure the chastening. Endure the rebuke. Endure the correction. If I am not applying the Word in Me, the Word will mean nothing. The Word needs to become flesh in you! He is the kingdom! He takes the kingdom of darkness out and puts His light inside of us! Are you going to water His Word or what?

How can a root come up? Because you water the seed! Now that thing is popping up and destroying everything around you. The blood of Jesus is a mind eraser! Let Him do it as you apply the Word of God. Bad seed produces bad weeds. Good seed produces a beautiful healthy garden.

Roots that come out of what Satan planted in you will trouble you. Bad roots will make you bitter. Weeds are bitter. God's word is organic and Truth. Whatever is not truth is a lie, even if it's true at that moment.

Water the God seed knowing that He loves you. God loves you because He loves you, but you don't believe. If you don't believe God loves you, nobody else will. If you don't have confidence in His love, you won't have confidence in somebody else's love for you.

The problem with being too quiet is that you can think a lot more. So if you are not talking to God, who are you talking to or thinking on? God or Satan? You will be having a conversation with the liar, and you will keep watering whatever seeds he throws in your garden, even using people from carnality and not the Spirit.

The peace of God shall keep your heart and mind in Christ Jesus. Whatever is pure, honest, just, lovely, of good report, praise, think on these things: what you have learned, received, heard and seen in those who are doers of the Word!

I don't care if how you felt at the moment was right. Repent! And pluck it out! Repent! Pluck it out!

Your peace comes from the seeds you water! His Word is spirit and life! What was the curse of Cain: You becoming a vagabond because of your rebelliousness, anger, and hate, with no presence of God. You will wander and will be homeless and absent of family.

He wants to see sons and daughters that walk in freedom and water the seed of God inside of them! The World has vagabonds and the religious system has them as well, but they all live in struggles. We are overcomers. Jesus blood cries out, "Forgiven!" If Abel's blood is still speaking, how much louder is the blood of Jesus?

All of us are tillers of the ground of our lives, and we all are called to feed one another. We are all called to be our brother's keeper. Bring the fruit of your heart; that means whatever you have been watering. Cain did what he was supposed to do, but his heart was full of weeds. God had no respect for it. His heart was wrong. We are now living sacrifices bringing ourselves to His holy altar!

If you water anger, anger will increase. Repentance makes you righteous. The curse of Cain was to become a vagabond, someone without a family, not having a spiritual family! We are to be having communion together! We need to be like Abel. How to do that? Weed your garden. Take care of the sheep.

Once God says something, it is done. It becomes law.

You will be walking, wishing you were dead when you are in rebellion, but that is not the life of God for us! We need to rip out every root that defiles us. We are called to be stable, and we need to be stable! We need to reach out and take hold of the horns of the altar and stop the enemy from sowing those seeds and stop watering them. When it first comes in, cast it down. Cast down every imagination or thought that comes against the Word of God (Truth).

Seed – Time = harvest! So you have time to pluck it out! Today!

You will be absent from the presence of the Lord if you don't!

Pray this: "Thank you, Father. We have a home and a family. We have the mind of Christ. You gave us power to pluck out every seed and not to meditate on any word that Satan has spoken or thrown seeds. You can't increase and decrease at the same time. Pull it out, Father, things that we don't have the strength to do it on our own. Give us grace, Father!

Father, we won't give idolatry to our emotions anymore. Father, right now, I rip every seed out of my heart that was not planted by My Father. Let the washing of the Word renew my mind. I know you. I know the same power that dwells inside of me. We are being changed even now, by the continuous washing and watering of the Word. Amen."

Let this mind be in you which is also in Christ Jesus. Think on things above, not below. Meditate on it. Water it. And you shall reap the harvest!

BREAKING BREAD Mark 4:3-34, Proverbs 23:1-21, Hebrews 12:10-17, Proverbs 18:21, Genesis 4:1-16

{

There is no birth without a push. Looking at people who are about to give birth to spiritual things can be so frustrating sometimes. You tell them to "push" and they don't push. You tell them to "breathe deep" and they don't. You tell them to "lie down" and they don't lie down. So they look at you waiting for an epidural, but you can't give it. Spiritual things have to be born in a natural way (without the hands of the flesh). The more they fight the pain, the more they suffer because it only increases from second to second. You can't stop her. Those impregnated by God get mad at you - thinking you don't care about their suffering - not understanding that the pain of childbirth is as necessary in the kingdom as it is in the natural. So sad to see people impregnated with God's things for years but never giving birth because they do not submit to pain (the cross) and their midwife (the Holy Spirit). So if you want to give birth to this baby, you must support the pain, follow the instructions, and when the time comes: "Push, Baby, push!"

Marlene Roessiger

"He answered and said unto them, Give ye them to eat."

Matthew 16:11

THE KINGDOM OF GOD IS LIKE

The Bible says that the Kingdom of God is like a lot of things. It uses examples to tell us that it is within us, and also it shows us how to make it grow, how to make it expand, and how to release it. Religion robs the living because it is dead. Theology without revelation of who and of now is dead. Nothing grows without life. Birthing, growing, and dying must occur in that order. That is how creation runs. God gives us creation to see His glory. Jesus defeated the second death so we can also live forever. So whatever is birthed in the natural will all die. The Kingdom of God will never die, neither will your spirit and soul to us who have been born again.

We keep birthing what God has placed inside of us: His seed. Let God continue to birth new things in us and around us that we will live forever. It just happens that God has birthed a baby in Brazil this year. Nine years of labor is birthing something stronger and greater in Brazil. Life starts at conception. And life starts with His Word! He spoke. It is conception.

Who is really speaking today by the Spirit of God? Who is going to prepare you for what is to come? Every person that thinks they are in the Kingdom and does not bring fruits of the Kingdom is not really of it! Any other fruit is birthed out of doctrines of man, you being your own God. New Age is filtering in the church, self-help, and self-motivation, but it is actually not His Kingdom. The Kingdom of God is a taking over of self.

The Gospel and the Holy Spirit are in the World to convince and convict us of sin, to change us. Jesus prayed to the Father what He wants to be done down here. His kingdom! His will be done! On Earth! In our lives!

Give us today our daily bread! Ask for your spiritual man to be filled! Don't ask for natural things. Deliver us from temptation! From the temptation of having itching ears. Preach and obey the Gospel of the Kingdom. In the real Gospel, you have to buy oil, you have to give up to gain, to die is to live.

When Jesus preached, demons manifested and they were cast out. In the religious system, demons manifested but they never go away. They stay where entertainment of the flesh is present. Are they preaching the Gospel of the Kingdom? Probably not. Jesus not only cast demons out, but He also charged them to never come back, and they never came back in some cases. The man dropped as dead had seen the power of God. We see this today in our meetings: from manifesting kundalini spirits and aggressive flailing and convulsing to the real thing, falling unto the power and the glory of God as one calm and dead but free, not in Word only – but in power!

Satan has no authority over your life unless you give power to Him. Some kinds of demons will never come out without relationship and sacrifice (fasting and prayer). We need to be close to Him and there will be a sign of the Kingdom: deliverance and freedom.

Sometimes the Kingdom of God does not look fair. "Why, God, is this so hard?" They start complaining. They feel weary. Everything He gives to you now is for eternity, but if you don't accept it, you walk out of His kingdom. Some people say, "We have been doing this for so long and nothing is happening," and they give up. You are looking to the wrong thing, comparing yourselves among yourselves. It is not wise. God keeps His Word and remembers your yes!

But did you not tell Him, "Come into my heart," and He is saying to you, "Come to My cross?" On the cross, you will see His kingdom, and you will enter in! Did you read, "Pick up your cross?" Did you read, "Forsake all?" Much is being given, much is required!

It works the same today! Repent! The kingdom of God is within, ahead, and is for now! How greater is He in you! Or how greater is he that is in the World? There is no other Gospel. He is expecting increase because the Kingdom of God is a kingdom ever increasing. His kingdom is opposite of the kingdom of the World. The last shall be first! The first shall be last!

If you think just because you are predestined you won't be left out, you are so wrong! You better do His will. You better not be a trouble maker to Him. You better walk in the narrow way. Remember: Only those who are predestined do. God has seen who are doers. You must be conformed.

The kingdom of God comes in a small size, but it takes over. It grows. It is always growing. God starts little and takes over. It is not for your job, your family, or yourself. It is all for His job and for His family. You are here to finish what He has started! Wake up! Be a son! Be a daughter! God sent more people to the vineyard, 3rd hour, 6th hour, 9th hour. He is the penny. He is the reward. Be steadfast. Don't be weary in well doing.

The Father, for His own good pleasure, decided to give to you the Kingdom! He delights in giving you the Kingdom!

Birthing. Growing. Dying. We all are supposed to live these three stages throughout our Christian walk. It has nothing to do with your process but with your surrendering. The Kingdom of God is not in bad shape. So let the Word of God sharpen you. You must be growing.

Many are called to work in the vineyard, but few are chosen. No one should be doing what you are supposed to do. Advance the Kingdom! Nobody really wants to do it His way because it takes a lot of dying, surrendering, and labor pains. The real Gospel works in power.

The Gospel of Jesus Christ will never be the number one bookseller when it's preached live! Nobody will want to pay the price for it. Anybody can buy a Bible, but to have it written in you, you will have to die! There is something about when the master spoke. It is so powerful! You can't deny the red letters. Serious Truth! Jesus is not a man that He could lie.

You have to be watchful as if a thief could come and break into your house any time of the day. We all need to take a nap sometimes. On which shift do you want to sleep? That is why we need each other: to watch and to pray. We need to keep each other awake! Don't be a gambler! Did He really mean what He spoke? Some people may question His hard words, "How can He be so loving and say these things?" But I am not going to reason with His Word, but believe. It is all the Truth! Every single Word He spoke! I need Him to do it!

There is still work to do! So much more to do! God is giving us the kingdom! Do you want to labor in the vineyard and get paid in the end? He is not a man that will rob you. He gives what He promised! It is going to be worth it all! Don't live for now! Don't build your own kingdom!

Many will be thrown in hell because they are not watching. You were living in the Kingdom but suddenly started building your own! The more Word inside of you, the more Word He is expecting out of you. The more presence in, the more presence out! The more oil in, the more oil out! The more money in, the more money out! He only expects you to give what He gives to you. No way out of it. Much is required of those who have the Kingdom inside of them!

There is a price. What do you mean? Jesus paid the price on the cross. Yes. Now you pay the price as well. Pick up your cross. Get your own oil. Obedience waters the kingdom of God! The disobedient live in a dry land! God is saying: "Obedience waters your kingdom seed and yielding brings growth."

Go back and look at all the parables about what the kingdom of God is like: Parables of farmers, fishermen, jewelers, businessmen, etc. This one thing He wanted all of us to understand and believe! Let us pay the price. Buy the field. Have peace, joy, and righteousness in Him. Let the Kingdom expand within you. See it. Water it. Manifest it! Let the World see what the Kingdom of God looks like!

BREAKING BREAD

Matthew 3, Matthew 6:9-15, Matthew 9:35-36, Matthew 12: 28-29, Matthew 13:31-33, Matthew 20:1-16, Luke 12:31-59

BOLDNESS

There is a big difference in claiming to know everything and really knowing everything: No man does! But what they do know they better act like they know it and preach it with all boldness. It's time for people who preach to preach what they know they that know and will die for it.

That is a religious coward who says I think or could be. Remember Jesus spoke as one having authority, not as the religious scribes and Pharisees (There is a huge difference, and if people are just used to hearing religious, orthodox-style preaching or man-pleasing, they tend to misjudge). What happened when Jesus, Paul, and Peter preached? Power broke out and disrupted communities. What happened when scribes and Pharisees spoke? People got confused and exalted them because they thought how amazing and so complicated it was and so deep. They had no clue what was said.

So, we don't know everything, but what we do know, we better know. Know Him and preach Him with boldness. If it is of God, He will back it. It's called authority, not pride. Was Jesus prideful? No! He spoke as one with authority. Religious spirits are still attacking that authority today. They see boldness as pride, but the righteous are as bold as a lion.

FORSAKE ALL

There was a rich guy that thought he was doing alright, but what was in his heart were his possessions: riches, family, job, sisters, brothers, fathers, children, wives, lands, and all the things he gained, the World. He heard the words of Jesus and thought, "I am a good candidate. I want to know how to obtain eternal life." He was full of self-righteousness! Then Jesus told him to sell and give away all you have and follow Me. Now Peter compared himself to the young ruler and said, "Hey, I have left all and what can I get in return?" Jesus said: "You that have left the religious system, the politics in the World, racism...they that left everything to follow Me, the real Truth, real love, real freedom, will receive your reward. But there is a cost!"

Do you remember in so many words Jesus said: "If you don't pick up your cross, you won't be worthy of me." He will ask you: "Did you obey me? Did you leave it all? Or did you compromise? Or did you ride on Balaam's horse? Or did you chase me for money or fame? Did you bow down to the prophets of Baal or to the gospel of prosperity (when I am everything)? Did you embrace the works of the Nicolaitans? Did you follow the narrow way? Did you make me first? When I have your heart, you will have My kingdom."

People need to pay the price for the anointing. Lay down your life. It is not about me laying my hands on your head, and you will be the anointing. Elisha followed Elijah. And we need to follow the Holy Spirit. Jesus will give us all. He will pour out His Spirit. Jesus has it all, way more than Elijah, and He will give all to us. Go buy oil! Jesus is saying: "Will you buy oil? Will you count the cost?"

The anointing will cost you everything, but we will have the keys to the Kingdom. When you follow Jesus, you will be hated by all men. You won't be pulled into politics. Politics in the church divides people, but the kingdom brings them together. We need to lay the right foundation of the kingdom of God. People will come, and they want to be part of whatever God is doing, but how many of them are willing to pay the price? How many are paying the price to stand on a firm foundation? How many are willing to pay the price for the anointing when demons shake when you walk in the room? Many will come like Simon, the sorcerer, thinking they can buy oil with earthly things. Obedience is better than sacrifice.

God is calling us to be faithful. He promised us 100%. NOW is this time! But we can't be looking at the return like Peter. When we started HOT in our house, we were not looking for a building or people, we were looking for Him, and He showed us the price we had to pay. We need to be looking for Him because if we don't, we will find anything else but HIM. The devil always wants leaven in the bread.

The last days are here. We are heading into dark times. Many mouths are talking about "Peace, peace," but Jesus warned us that great destruction is ahead of us. We are houses that will hear what the Spirit is saying to the church, not what the political party is saying, or what the anti-Christ spirit is saying, but what the spirit of Truth is saying to us right now. The great apostasy is coming! The falling away when your brothers, sisters, mothers, your own family will turn you into the authorities because you are not deceived like them. You are hearing the Spirit of Truth. God is building spiritual houses (you) where His presence will dwell there! Because the kingdom of God is inside of us, and we will release it into the atmosphere!

All that Jesus has for us will come with PERSECUTION. You have not seen anything yet. You are being persecuted now just because you have decided to follow Jesus, but the level of persecution is not to compare with what is to come. You need to make sure that your foundation is the rock - Jesus Christ.

The greatest move of God is about to happen, but who is willing to pay the price? The anointing will cost you everything. Persecution! Being hated by your brothers and sisters! They will hate the Gospel of Jesus. People love the TV preachers because they are not preaching it. The TV preachers focus on you and on what Jesus did two thousand years ago, but that is half the history. We need to know what He is doing now. He did not die on the cross and rise to be about only that but to give you authority, to give you a sword, to give you boldness, to give you power, and to multiply Himself, so that He will be known and still be working on the Earth for His glory. People have a false agreement with when He said, "It is finished." Then they think that they don't need to do anything. This is the biggest lie from religion because it comes against all the other scriptures.

He said, "It is finished and I did everything as a forerunner. Now you will be able to follow Me and do all I have done and greater works: salvation, transformation, and acceleration concerning advancing the kingdom in you." The World is waiting. They don't even know it, but you do. This is why I hate religion. It does not multiply. It does not advance.

Jesus was preaching to the crowd until He started talking about "drink His blood, eat His flesh." In **John 6:66**, many disciples were not walking with Him anymore, and Jesus said: "Are you going to leave me too, Peter?" Peter said "Where will I go? You only have the Words of life." Some can't handle the words of life. That is why they stay dead. The Word of life needs to be done. He is the Word, and we are the doers. He has already done it now in you and me.

The latter rain shall be greater! "I will build My church and the gates of hell will have no power over it. Seducing spirits will not seduce them anymore. Jezebel will not be preaching at the altar. It is always going to be My Spirit in man, in men and women that are counting the cost." Then don't expect many to want what you want. It does not matter how many people are gathering with you. Obey the call!

The World is laughing, not at the real Jesus, but at the hypocrites and those who call themselves Christians, but you found them as liars. His church, His house, the tabernacle of David, the apostolic church, will cast out demons, heal the sick, raise the dead and preach the Gospel to the poor. We will be doing ONLY what the Father is doing.

Can you drink the cup? Can you drink it? You know about the cup, but can you drink it and be baptized into the baptism of the dead? Everybody says, " We can," but when He hands you the cup: the cup of persecution, the cup of your family hating you, the cup of people talking behind your back, the cup of mocking, of laying down your life, the cup of turning the other cheek, the cup of loving your enemies, or the cup of being the sheep led to the slaughter, you really don't drink it. You say yes, but you don't swallow it or drink it with joy!

Drink the cup of love! It is easy to love those who love you. The World does that. God wants us to love those who hate us. Can you drink this cup? Nobody can accuse the doctrine I preach, but they will always try to find a fault in the messenger. They lied about Stephen. They lied about Jesus. They lie about you when what you are doing is living by the Truth. Can you drink the cup of people lying about you?

We are not a denomination or the next movement. We are the bride of Christ. We are followers of the cross: under the glory of God and the apostolic order of God, drinking His blood, eating His flesh, having Him put His life in us, taking up our cross, and we are our new identity. Wake up, sleeping giants!

What Paul says, "I am not who I was. I am crucified. I no longer live but Christ lives in me." It is not you living anymore but Christ. Jesus did not die on the cross for us to join a social club - the "bless me" club. All the blessings are already ours when we obey the Truth. Everything is ours when we forsake all.

Do you want to take the cup of what minister really means? Minister means to serve. Everybody wants to have a ministry without taking the cup. Before you grab the microphone, you need to serve. Jesus is our master example. The greatest leader of all! The greatest servant of all! Do you want to be the greatest? Be the servant of all - that is another cup to drink.

Do you want to take the cup of leaving your mother and father? "Well, but Jesus preaches love. He preaches about honoring your father and mother." So what is He saying? He needs to be first, even above them. Loving people does not mean that you don't honor them. A man's foes will release you to the authorities (**Matthew 10:36**). What if they are against the will of the Father? You need to honor the Father above them! If your household is not going where Jesus is, then you are going in the wrong direction.

If you try to keep your life, you always will lose it. This is the type of preaching that the crowd hated. They will tell you that you are part of a cult! What an honor! The rock of offense became the rock of the foundation of the church that we are part of today. Jesus is filling the Earth with His doctrine and His Spirit, and the Pharisees and Sadducees could not deny the works done by Jesus. They thought if His doctrine is not prospering, it is not of God. But guess what? His doctrine is prospering still today!

The dead are always burying the dead. Why are you looking for the living among the dead? Why are you looking for Me in a dead system? It is time to forsake the system. God is alive! Follow Him! Life and death don't live in the same place.

God is causing a massive exodus out of tradition, religion, paganism, a self-centered lifestyle, works of Nicolaitans, doctrines of Balaam, and out from under teachings of Jezebel. We need to hate what He hates. We are here, but we are not of this World. We are pilgrims! We are separated by Him! He wants you to be the church of Philadelphia. Doors wide open!

He is not coming for a denomination but for a bride full of oil that pays the price with her own life! You can't live off my oil. You need to get your own.

Today, pay the price for following Jesus and His Word! If you love Him, die for Him. There is no greater love than this: to lay down your life for Him, not for a sect, denomination, or anything but for His own sake, and when He possesses you and shows you the way of life, you will know that there is nothing else worth living for. This is the Gospel that the Spirit of Elijah is preaching.

Are you ready to follow Him and forsake all? To see things you have never seen before? To go places you have never gone before? Decide today to pay whatever the price may be. He is worthy of it all! The oil is the light and you must trim your wick daily because He is coming soon. Will He find you doing it?

"Then answered Peter and said unto him, Behold, we have forsaken all, and followed thee; what shall we have therefore? And Jesus said unto them, Verily I say unto you, That ye which have followed me, in the regeneration when the Son of man shall sit in the throne of his glory, ye also shall sit upon twelve thrones, judging the twelve tribes of Israel. And every one that hath forsaken houses, or brethren, or sisters, or father, or mother, or wife, or children, or lands, for my name's sake, shall receive an hundredfold, and shall inherit everlasting life. But many that are first shall be last; and the last shall be first." Matthew 19:27-30

BREAKING BREAD

Mark 10:28-45, Matthew 10:32-42, Matthew 8:19-23

"And when Jesus knew, he saith unto them, Why reason ye, because ye have no bread? perceive ye not yet, neither understand? have ye your heart yet hardened?"

Mark 8:17

HOW TO HEAR THE VOICE OF GOD

Some people say, "How do I know it is God?" We all should know the voice of our Father. There is the known will of God which is written in the Word. The unknown will of God is revealed to every single one of us in a personal way. For example: marry this one, live here, do this, and that, but in both cases, when we were told to do something and we didn't do it, we can end up in the belly of a big fish. Some are blaming the devil, but where they are right now could be the fruit of their disobedience.

Sometimes, God tells you to do something and you don't. Then you end up in the belly of the big fish and you think it is the devil, but then he is tormenting you. It is pride when we blame the devil because we don't take responsibility.

Pivotal things and decisions we do and make by the will of God. In His will, there is peace and joy. Some people live out of the will of God, and they go back to misery, drugs, and distress. Backsliding is the result of not keeping and obeying God, and people will end up in a place that they never intended to be. This is why obedience is where the healing is.

We should know right in the minute that someone speaks from God if they are really from God or not. This is our portion, not to be tossed, but you will never know if you are not in relationship with the Spirit and the Word.

The only time we can blame the devil is when you are possessed by him because you don't have control, but for him to do that, you would have had to do a lot of rebellion and fellowship with darkness. God is using elements of the World to bring you to humility. The written Word cannot lead to personal decision but to righteousness! The Bible does not say marry so and so, or live here or there, but it keeps us on the path of God so we live in no confusion or divination. Then the steps of the righteous are ordered.

Our choices determine our future. Some people may say when they are on the wrong path: "God is teaching me something." Yes, He is. He is teaching you to listen and to obey what He is saying. His heart is to have relationship with us. We were created to hear our shepherd if we are a sheep, not through a pastor only or a book.

The known will of God is for us all, but when we bring the Word, they say, "No, no, this is not for me." When you get out of the will of God, you stop hearing Him. "Where are you, God?" He says: "I am right here where you left me. Come back to the path of righteousness!" When we are in the light, we see Him and hear Him. We have given our ear to many wolves and hirelings and our ears to their doctrines. We have given our ears to our own god as well, our own desires and lusts. That's why Jesus says return to Me. Deception makes us think that we are what we are not. His voice is our compass.

We are each other's doorkeeper as well! We watch over each other. Others will come and will speak, but they are the voice of the stranger! We should recognize the voice of the stranger! If you obey God, the devil cannot touch you, but he will if you do not forgive, if you do not obey when God tells you to, and if you do not turn left when He points it to you. A lot of our storms are created by ourselves because our will is the strong will. Our way is an easy way. He has better plans for you than you ever will. We have promises in the Word of God. Every one of them comes with the price of obedience. This is why sound doctrine is very important.

Hear the voice of God for yourself. For example, He said, "Stay in Jerusalem until you receive power," but you also go and do everything He said in **Mark 16**, "Go and preach the Gospel." So, the Word of God says both: wait and go! God uses the Word for directions as well as by illumination, showing one thing by the Spirit, and your spirit bears witness.

If it is the voice of God, your spirit will recognize it right away. The Word is alive, meaning for you now. If you are getting confused, you need more discernment. Satan is the father of confusion. That is why having a really strong spiritual body and family around us helps us to discern His voice. When we walk out of the light, it is almost impossible to hear God, but He will use a donkey if need be. God uses the Word to renew our mind and light our way. He will never tell us to do something against His Word and His own will, which is righteousness.

When He said, "This is your wife. Marry her," your spirit confirms that that voice was the voice of your Father and so will the Body of Christ. This is why Satan loves to scatter us or send us into the World or solo through offense and pride, but from Genesis to Revelation, God says, "Come out!"

The one that breaks the sheep's legs is not the devil but the shepherd. He will do anything to bring you back to His safe place. My freedom is in staying with my Father. My God is holy. He says, "Be holy as He is." What true love really looks like: God chastens the ones He loves. Love doesn't say do what you want—that is false love. Some people don't tell the sheep Truth because they love popularity. They seduce sheep for money and a following because they love themselves more than God.

Everybody is running for a word from the prophet because they are not hearing His voice anymore on their own. His sheep always hear His voice. Why do we hear Him? Because we are His sheep! He said, "My sheep hear My voice," not may or could.

Some say: "Tell me plainly. I don't understand," and the Lord is saying: "I did." But we believe not! Those that are not following the Word may not be His sheep. Few shall follow Him! Few shall follow the Word. Many followed Him no more because His Words were too hard, but many are saying, "Where should I go? Only you have the Words of life!" The Holy Spirit will never come against His own Word. How do you know that it is not of God? Because my spirit always bears witness with the Truth! What is Truth? Jesus is the Word. You follow the Word, and you will be able to be led by the Spirit and be hidden in the perfect will of God.

Don't rely on dreams and visions or revelatory gifts only, but don't despise them either. Just follow Him, His Word. The minute you are out of His will, you will know it. God corrects us by people out in the World beating us up, by dryness, and by the way things get hard. He will use anything to chastise us all. If you are apostles but are rebellious, you will spend your entire life in your living room doing nothing. It is not our calling that blesses us. It is our obedience! We all are His sheep. We all have Him, and He is faithful. All of His promises are for all His sheep, and they are yes and amen!

It is not wise to measure yourself among yourselves! Measure yourself to Christ, and you will stay always in that lower place. Let Him exalt you! The porter (the gatekeeper, the seers) opens the door, and the Spirit leads them into the Shepherd! Peter heard the Father clearly because He was His sheep. Peter did not get it from man. The Father Himself gave that to Him because

Peter was part of His fold. Jesus said, "You did not get this from flesh and blood." So, we all have access when we follow the shepherd, the living Word.

"Feed My sheep." Don't feed the goats or the wolves! "Feed His sheep." Those who listen to His voice; those that follow Him. God has appointed people to protect His own. If you are not gathering, you are scattering. Jesus is gathering people unto His Father. There are many sheep caught up among the wolves. The good shepherds go there and rescue them all! Real love lays down his life to follow the Lamb wherever He goes.

Nobody is born into God from natural birth. Everybody has to go through the cross, eat the lamb, repent, and be born again. Then you enter in! No self-help can help you enter in. So if you use these carnal new age formulas, it means that you need to help yourself because God can't help you anymore? No courtroom in heaven can help a disobedient son and daughter. In Christ, we are free. Don't let religion separate you from Him with steps and formulas and rituals.

If you are really of God, you would love Truth because Jesus is Truth. Jesus always restores our souls. Our spirits are not victims or have any wounds, but our souls do. When you hear His voice, you get restoration. The glory of His presence will do it! He is a healer! When you really hear God, people try to make you confused, asking you, "Do you really hear Him?" "Are you sure?" If you are a sheep, you will hear your shepherd. If not, you will hear another. His sheep will follow His written Word.

God is giving us all discernment to recognize the voice of the stranger immediately. We should never follow it. Satan is like, "Let's hope they will never get hold of the Truth!" But we have it! We eat it! We follow it! We don't get offended at it! No matter what it sounds like, we know the sound if we stay in the Word.

The prodigal son in his father's house heard his voice every single day until he decided to do his will, his lust! It was when he wanted what he wanted for a season. His freedom was fun for a minute, but eventually, he ended up with the swine. Go back to the Father's house. He has a robe, a ring, and a big hug for you. Don't waste another day!

Many don't know what they are doing, and God is saying, "Repent! Seek Me and repent!" God is a God of infinite chances. Hear Him. Follow His voice. Obey it!

The voice of the stranger can be speaking words to your personal situation from the Bible - out of context - but they don't come from the Father or the Spirit. Just because someone posts scripture does not mean it's His voice for you now.

We want to follow only the Father's voice! Dine with Him! Sit with Him! Father, open our eyes! Jesus in us all should bear witness of the Truth. This is for now! Every one that is of the Truth hears His voice! Pilate and many are asking: "What is Truth?" Look at Jesus. He is the Truth. Hear Him.

If you are of Truth, you are His sheep, and surely you will hear His voice! No matter what, if you are the older brother or the wayward, He has all we need. Obedience is the key to breakthrough, not a meeting at a conference, not a "Hearing God's Voice" series for $49.99. "Lord, help us! Father, open our eyes and ears. Show us. Heal us and deliver us. We were born to live in our Father's house and to hear clearly the voice of the Father.

BREAKING BREAD Psalm 119:104-106, John 10:1-30, John 8:30-59, John 12:35-50, John 18:37-38

HIS WORDS ARE
LIKE LIGHTHING

As you read this you will understand the importance of the black and the white (no compromising) and the prophetic unction. Many come against the apostolic, but they are in error because they say God will do a new thing. But every day, all the time, He is doing a new thing. When Jesus came, it was a new thing, a new covenant, and a new way. Although He never changes, times and seasons do. Although there are many false apostolic movements, there still is a real bride and a real church that God is raising up, and it will run by fivefold ministers ordained by God, not man. It won't be run by board members and denominations. This church casts out demons.

This church will have no spots or wrinkles when Jesus comes, even though Satan is taking the revelation of the apostolic and perverting it in many places because they won't give up Balaam or the works of the Nicolaitans. The apostolic will uproot all the old wine, but they keep mixture. They stay pagan. But a bunch of wolves are trying to say the apostolic is not from God. The funny thing is that God is a God of order, God is repairing the gates, and God is raising up His Church. The problem with these religious zealots is they are very critical. They throw the baby out with the bath water. They have no power. They can't cast out demons. All they do all the time is try to find all the negative when God says look at all the fruit. The book of Jude is for them. His church will be a living organism as the body moves by the meat coming on the bones as Ezekiel has prophesied. This is the time. See, religion is an antichrist spirit of Cain that wants to kill the apostolic which is Christ. As we expose darkness and error and dead works, they attack like Pharisees what music you listen to or what words you use.

We must have mercy, but you better not be blaspheming the Holy Spirit. I tell you this: They are causing confusion because they are speaking some truth without any Spirit. Everything God gave Paul will come to pass. Meat coming on the bones is the HOLY SPIRIT coming on His bride. God said, "This day, THIS DAY, you will begin to see this spirit that is bringing witchcraft on hungry sons and daughters." Confusion is not from the HOLY SPIRIT. You will begin to see and feel and realize, wow, why now am I questioning my direction? Why now am I feeling afraid? This is the voice of a stranger! GOD IS RAISING UP HIS BRIDE! IT IS MARVELOUS. God is separating all the children of disobedience, those who kick against the pricks. Watch, things will become clear! Our Spirit bears witness that we are sons of God and that we are in one accord, one doctrine, one faith, and one love. Even if we are not all in the same revelation or on the same level, we can still be in one accord unless we are a goat. It does not matter. There is no division in TRUTH, GRACE, AND LOVE. Let God keep separating everyone who will hinder His power and plans.

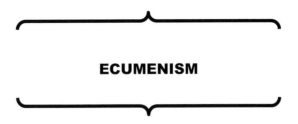

ECUMENISM

THE ECUMENISM MOVEMENT IS NOT OF GOD!

Noun: ecumenism – the principle or aim of promoting unity among the world's Christian churches.

Definition of ECUMENISM – Ecumenical principles and practices especially as shown among religious groups (as Christian denominations)

Webster's dictionary: Ecumenism: the movement or tendency toward worldwide Christian unity or cooperation. The term, of recent origin, emphasizes what is viewed as the universality of the Christian churches.

THIS IS NOT OKAY, CHURCH...This is one of the seven mountains that she, the HARLOT of Babylon, is sitting on. This false unity is the forerunner to one world religion. Don't let them suck you in. Know what is happening in the mainstream church in America and abroad today. Because of false definitions of God and His love, we are seeing before our eyes the apostasy, the falling away, right before our eyes. First, they distort doctrines and then you can distort the minds and hearts of people. Blind leaders are leading blind people, perverting God's love, leaving hell and repentance and a list of Jesus' teachings out of their doctrines and sermons, sugar coating denying oneself. Jesus is the Way, the Truth, and the Life. False prophets and teachers twist the love of God and pervert the Gospel. They have a name and fame so many listen. These cowards are perverting the Gospel and holding hands with the devil. Paul says to rebuke them sharply. That's what God's prophets are doing. They will tell you Elijah is supposed be a coward like they are, man-pleasing, and telling you what they think modern day prophets are supposed to look like. These err from the faith, giving over to seducing spirits and doctrines of devils. We need to put this out on Christian TV. These are man-pleasers...They are bowing to the anti-Christ spirit as well as many mainstream preachers today. It's time to blow the trumpet.

These movements of prayer and coming together are a waste of time if your foundation is not on the rock. Always who's who. GOOD or GOD. Everything that seems good is not God. When the Holy Spirit fell, they were all in one mind, one accord, and one SPIRIT, not just in one place. This one place thing is a distraction and a lie. Holy Spirit is not divided. A house like that cannot stand. We must be in one Spirit and in one Truth. There is no such thing as putting our differences aside. It's called false unity. Jesus said He has come not to bring peace but division, dividing us to HIS PURE WORD and PURE DOCTRINE without a denominational twist of opinions, rules, membership, additions, and philosophies of man! The Holy Spirit guides us into all Truth. Those who are baptized in that fire, in that Truth, are not deceived. There is also a counterfeit Holy Spirit out there posing as the real one. False healing and false manifestations...HOLY SPIRIT is holy when we encounter Him. The first thing He does is convict us of sin and bring us to repentance. He must first be our converter before He is our comforter. I am speaking loud and clear. Your compromise has come up before the throne. Jezebels and false voices will be thrown to the sick bed as we have seen many dying for lying. All those who commit spiritual fornication with her will as well. We have another anti-Christ activity. God and His Holy Spirit will not promote false doctrine or false unity. These prayer gatherings are coming from religion and the anti-Christ spirit. THE RIGHTEOUS ARE AS BOLD AS A LION. I tell you that this is what needs to be happening to the pope and to every other false religion or doctrine of devils: They need to get saved. Woe to anyone who would not tell them otherwise or turn away. YOU ARE AN ANTI-CHRIST – that's the spirit in you. They are not of God unless they have deceived themselves already. HEAR ME CLEARLY: CATHOLICISM AND JESUS HAVE ZERO AGREEMENT, as does any idolatry religion that is praying to statues, exalting man, and praying to dead people. You are deceived. Even Satan believes Jesus is the only way. Jesus said you know my disciples by their fruit. They call themselves Christians, but they are the synagogue of Satan. Why in the world do I have to ask them for forgiveness? This is crazy to bow and to kiss the feet OF A MAN.

PRIEST JESUS IS THE ONLY ONE WE BOW TO! Messengers of deception! WAKE UP, CHURCH! Crazy stuff! I tell you to run for your life. God has led these leaders to be deceived because they are eating at the harlot's table holding back the Truth. Why am I so zealous? Because of you! They have lots of money. They have lots of influence. Christian television, Christian radio, magazines, and followers all over the world are being deceived and don't even know it. The good ones of yesterday are now coming under her seduction!! IN THE FEAR OF THE LORD, I stand.

BREAKING BREAD

Luke 12:49-53, 2 Timothy 4:2-4, Titus 2:15, Titus 1:9-16

What I consider blessing others may see as something else! Blessing to me is true friends, favor, anointing, loyal people around me, hungry people around me, His presence around me at all times, His peace and joy, truth and hearing His voice. Blessing to me is to be full of hope and faith!

....

Wolves follow the voice of a stranger. The voice of Truth they will resist. They will gather the goats from the four winds. They will build a synagogue of Satan. They will get a reprobate mind. They will back and fight for position and fame! They will turn the grace of God into shame and false freedom. The apostate church is their name, void of the fear of the Lord. Let us run the race and keep enduring until the end.

"And when one of them that sat at meat with him heard these things, he said unto him, Blessed [is] he that shall eat bread in the kingdom of God."

Luke 14:15

THE PRICE FOR THE ANOINTING

Your foundation has to be sound. You were predestined to be conformed, but you are only formed into what you are planted in! If you are planted into a system, you will be conformed into that system. If you are planted in the world, you will become worldly. There are churches popping up like popcorn, but this is not from God. He has already planted the way, the truth, and the life. If you change a structure ordained by God, you are building on hay, wood, and stubble. If you are building on sand, it will fall. Many are in competition trying to be the coolest church, the most non-pressure church, or the most relevant church. All this is works of the flesh. The craziest thing is that a church is not a place or a gathering. It is a living organism, not an organization. It is supposed to look like what it represents. Funny, you are supposed to be a pastor. Then you were one ever since you were born again. Church is not an opportunity. It's a call. So is being part of a ministry or a tribe. One day you were a traveling minister working from a gift, now you rent a building and call a meeting. Now Satan gives you a title of pastor. This is works of Nicolaitans, and Balaam will not be advancing God's agenda but their own. Church is not a "good idea." It has a divine nature. If you are not an apostle, you can't start anything but your car. I'm telling people we need to get this thing together and fast.

When you follow God, you need to pay a price for the anointing of God. We are releasing vision to leaders. Many are called and few are chosen. Man cannot choose you. That is what's going on in the emerging puke. It is out of order. God will spew it out of His mouth. It will speak at the end. God is not mocked. We reap what we sow. It's not a good idea, not a marketing Jesus industry. It's a mandate from heaven. You better follow His blueprints. Everyone in the Church of Jesus Christ will not be welcomed, will not be relevant, will not be accepted, will not be popular, and will not be competition. The church of the Holy Spirit does not move in the flesh, does not hold hands with the world, does not worry about having the best coffee and fastest service, and does not say it is low pressure. The anointing cost everything. The anointing puts a demand on the flesh all the time. It does not promote only fellowship. It promotes the cross where we are called to die!

This word will tell you what the Word of God says about the church!! God is apostolic. He is not like us nor does it draw men by the works of the flesh or better opportunities. He does not market his possessions. We are His. He rebukes, corrects, edifies, and changes us from faith to faith, word to word, and glory to glory. You are only predestined if you pick up your cross, not if you join a club. God has been turning man over to deception because they want to bring false TRUTH, GRACE, AND LOVE. This is apostasy, and many want the easy way. He said my way will be the hardest way, but it will be glorious, and it will speak. ECCLESIASTIC is not man's idea but God's. So many are OUT OF ORDER! Do not be drunk with wine, but be filled with the Spirit!! God is very, very concerned for His government to be established!

The end time church is supposed to be more powerful and more glorious, not more carnal. Let this revelatory message blow your mind because the mind of Christ is the only mind. That mind will be the will of God. Don't let yourself be marketed or merchandised! There are two directions that the church is going. What direction are you going? Examine yourself whether you are really in the faith.

{

He is Lord of lords and the King of kings! All who become without can only be who and what is within! God says He has never seen the "righteous" forsaken or their seed begging for bread. God says, "You judge Me because you don't know Me. If you knew Me, you would be blessed!" Remnant, we are not called to live in the wilderness. Yes, God has brought many into it. You may be there now, but we are supposed to go through it. Anyone who lives there is someone who refuses to let God change them. I don't care where you live, what you have done, and how people hurt you or abused you. We all have that. But He is no respecter of persons. Your mountain may be bigger than most, but then He is bigger. He even has that much more grace. Victims depend on man. Victors depend on God. Trust Him. Obey and follow him. We are either overcomers or we are overcome. Don't let Satan lie to you that you have a right. Know that when you don't believe God, it is sin, no matter how big the giants are. Do not let pity sneak in and allow worldly mentality to steal your land. Repent for your ugliness and bitterness and cut off your critical spirit first. Then rise up and take your land by force! Many will not like this because now they will be accountable. You can't blame God or others if you are His.

EXPOSING OR SLANDERING

Let me show you what God showed me. The more you speak the Truth, the more the religious spirit will want to kill you! Judas hated the Truth so he came in agreement with the spirit of hate (murder) and hypocrisy. A true sign of negative agreement is when we have hidden agendas and suddenly we start gathering with some people in the Body trying to change their thinking, making them to believe that things should be different when they are exactly the way God wants. A fertile ground for negative agreement is when we meet someone that is as jealous as we are and are full of envious for attention and for position in the Body.

The Bible says if there is a divisive person among you, mark him as a brother but have nothing to do with them. This spirit of religion loves to judge, not according to love and truth in the Spirit, but according to what they believe. They do not take biblical steps when mad or offended because of pride. They never get offended in their mind because that is not what perfect people do. This spirit loves to attack what God is exalting like Cain says, "What about me?" Cain was religious. His brother, Abel, was righteous. You cannot be both. That's why Judas stabbed Jesus in the back because he was not in love with Jesus. It was not a sin that Jesus did it pure. This religious spirit has a hate for truth and for submission. It brought envy and hate for truth. The more Godly and honorable you become, the more attack is on the way.

Religious people will look to slander you because you are becoming more desirable than they are. Also, the closer they are to you, the more dangerous they can become because now they think they have supernatural insight on you and know your weaknesses and that they know better than other people about you. They get very familiar. When they turn on you, people will turn with them because of the same familiar spirit. They hate that you expose Satan so they slander you. You could be doing 98% perfectly or right, but all they tell others, mostly in secret, is the 2% that they have on someone, not even sin, just flesh and flaws. It's all belief differences that bring these rats out. God hates division and discord. They bring divination to make you think God said something or showed them some secret things about you, but it's all in their imagination because their heart is dark.

The other big thing is that religious people will accuse you of doing the very same thing they are doing — that twister twisting positions. They never come to ask why you do or say something because they have already decided they are the only ones right in their minds. They own an island, and they are king, prophet, and ruler of their own making, becoming their own god. It's a spirit of Cain. They attack prophets mostly because of their compromise and refusal to repent for evil in their heart. There is a big difference with bashing, slander, gossip, backbiting, dissension, discord, and false accusing than a minister exposing general error and the devil and preaching Truth.

These wolves will find each other. God said to me, the minute you begin to give an ear to divisive people, you come in agreement with that spirit and become divisive yourself. Look at the world right now. We have never been this divided since the Civil War. Why, because they feel they have a right. One side thinks they are right. When you feel right and wrong you begin to lose your mind. It's called anarchy, and it's out of control, and you become a reprobate to the Word of God. You become lawless, just like the world. You, as a Christian, have two laws to follow: God's law and the law of the land (if it does not cause you to break God's law first). You do not live by God's words or standards but actually, exalt yourself above the Word of God, and in your puffed-up mind, you believe God is for what you are doing, and that is deception. We must stay in love and in the Word. Then you say you love God and hate your brother and your old good friend and stab him or her in the back. God says you're deceived and don't lie and say you love me. You must love whether you're right or you're wrong. It was when you turned from the narrow way. There is a way that God exposes lies. It's with Truth and the Spirit, not with accusation and slander in your private messenger. Well, I tell you nothing is private to God. He sees it all. He will expose every secret and lie by the Light. The mature guard their hearts. Life is way too important to them than being right. How are you ever going to love your enemies when you can't even love someone who has loved you for a while? This is one area that God does not play around with – slander. Speaking truth in love is the only way God exposes anything off in the body. So get off your religious high horse before God knocks you off. Demonizing the saints is not a good idea. Ask Judas. It will eventually turn on you. You murder yourself and your destiny, and you will be marked. Repent. Let God be God. You are not made for that position. Or you will end up in a camp where all they do is criticize, judge, and accuse. We are called to bring life not death.

{

Gossip is sin, whether you are the one doing it, or you are the one listening to it – it takes two! It's gossip unless all parties are present when you want to tell someone something about another, especially a body member! You better rebuke that person and run because Satan will deceive you! Tale-bearers and backbiters are all works of Satan! Let us walk in the Spirit and the Truth! Let not Satan use you to get people out of love and the truth and the will of God! You can only weep and mourn for Saul for a minute. Then God says, "Get up! Get moving, David!" I am so seriously sad and cannot believe the things that I hear coming out of people's hearts and mouths. Shocked!

"And it came to pass, as he sat at meat with them, he took bread, and blessed it, and brake, and gave to them."

Luke 24:30

WHAT DO YOU NEED?

God is saying: we live in a world of need, but in the Kingdom, the only thing we need is to be led by the Spirit. The world moves by need. One thing we do, religiously, is to move by what we need as well. Everybody needs salvation, everybody needs healing, but Jesus did not run to all of their needs.

Jesus never moved by our need, never by our wanting. It was faith that moved Him. He walked by hurting people. He only preached long when there were ears to hear.

If we are being moved by our need, then we can't be led by Him. Jesus was always moved by the Spirit. Jesus was moved with compassion but not led by it. He was led by the Spirit because the Spirit had compassion on people, but the Spirit knew the heart of man and God's timing.

If we are led by the Spirit, we also will be rejecting some people, just like Jesus did. Satan will send you needy people all the time. These could be a distraction. The kingdom of God is not by observation.

Someone said: "Enoch walked with God and some people only walk with their Bible." You need to walk with God to be led by God and not by the written letter only. All that produces is a hit or miss lifestyle of doing dead works.

You can be seeking Him but not obeying Him. Religious seek, seek, seek, but they never have it, but His bride was found by Him and she keeps Him and keeps connected to Him. She walks with Him in that. She is being led by Him. Religion is always led by the letter. One is a way of life. The other is something we do during the day.

Sometimes people talk about a "salvation message," making an altar call for salvation every time they speak or preach when in your spirit you already know the listeners are all saved already. How do you know? My spirit told me. So you were being led by a blanket need and the letter but not by the Spirit. Needs produce traditions, so then you are led by your own practices and styles and works.

When all you have is knowledge, you can't see the kingdom of God. The more you are changed and like Him, the more you feel alone. It is called the separation of the bride. You can't be manipulated by anything. You keep guarding your heart. That is why religion stabilizes their souls by the works for the needs. The Spirit rests in knowing He is pleased and walking in Him.

Wherever Jesus went, demons manifested. They never understood that Jesus manifested because of the glory He carried and not because He was of the devil. Today religion will say, "You have demons," because when the anointing is there, they manifest. What we really have is the anointing. There is also false deliverance that talks to demons. This could be a demon confusing a believer or putting on a show. Jesus' deliverance ministry did not make a display or a show, but they just came out! Just because you talk to a demon does not make a person delivered. Demons are liars. I have cast out thousands of demons and never had a conversation with one, only heard people screaming. When the glory is present, demons can't even handle the heat. They manifest, not have fellowship. There is a lot of deception out there. Jesus one time asked a demon a question. He did not fight the demon. The demon was in total submission.

I make a plan, but when the wind blows, I am flowing with it! The highest way goes beyond good, but totally God. God is good, but good does not always mean it is God! Some people are following their own need. Step aside. Let God's grace do the work.

God told them to sing, and they go beyond and start preaching. Let the preacher preach! Let the singer sing. We need to stop making celebrities from gifts. Hollywood Christian TV is making many famous, and they are losing the anointing when they man-please.

The kingdom of God is not what we see but is the trail of where we have been. If you seek manifestation, you will never see His kingdom. Signs will follow us. It's not our place to follow them.

Here are the needs the world seeks: Need for food. We all need to eat, but the Word tells us not to let our belly rule, and also says His kingdom is not a matter of food or drink, but of what? Also, says God, He will take care of you if you follow Him.

People bear witness with John because John bore witness of Jesus. If we all bear witness with each other, that is a sign that we all bear witness of His Spirit. Just because they talk about Him does not mean they know Him. The devil talks about Him, from Revelation and Genesis, Greek, Hebrew, whatever, you will never get to know Him from just reading about Him! All we need is to know Him by the Spirit!

A man can't receive anything except what is given to him from heaven! He that comes from above is above all. The system of the World operates in need! For example, the need for education, money, or careers. In the World, your needs never stop. Need for a car. You need "a this" to get "a that." In the kingdom, all we need is Him!

My God shall supply all your need, NOT according to your wants, but according to His riches in glory by Christ Jesus. For those who trust Him, obey Him. The religious keep operating by need all the time. Humanitarianism! They like to live by their need, and they are never satisfied! They like to do a lot of things to be needed. Then they like people to see them. They like to be needed, and they are always fulfilling needs.

God really does not need us but He made a need for us.

Our knowledge about their need can't cause us to move. Then we are moving by sight and not by the Spirit. We can't go ahead of Him. Need is everywhere! What do we do? We wait on Him and only move when He moves. When we focus on needs, we can't focus on the Spirit. You become ritualistic, and you can't ever be led by the Spirit. You can't be led by scripts or formulas. They always have the need around, the poor around, or the lost around. All need something, but Jesus only did what He saw the Spirit doing.

Jesus got led to that man by the pool by the Spirit. There was a specific moment. Sometimes we get frustrated because we are moving, doing what He called us to do, but we are moving by the need or our zeal. Many are filled with the Holy Spirit, but they are not being led by it. We can't do anything on our own unless we see the Father doing it.

Whatever we see Him doing, we do. If He ignores a need, we ignore a need as well because He must be concerned with something else at that time, or He is doing something else to the needy or to another. Just because you have a healing gift does not mean you run when you feel like it to the hospital and heal everyone.

It might be the Truth but by another spirit: the spirit of divination. In the desert, Satan, looking to satisfy Jesus' need, spoke the Truth back to Jesus, but Jesus spoke Truth with the Spirit and overcame that lie. Saying something true but from another spirit is divination. The source will direct the course.

A lot of people honor God but never mention the Son or the Holy Spirit. If we don't honor three in one, we are not honoring God at all. Then ignoring the Spirit in one another, even when we do good, can be in the way of God.

When He is all that you want, you will have all that you need. Humility gets everything from heaven. Humanity gets everything from man.

Religious kills everything. It is murder. It will kill your relationship with God, will kill your friends, and your joy, until the point that you commit spiritual suicide. Religious does what religious does but can't ever follow the Spirit. It follows patterns, formulas, and tradition.

God told us to preach the Gospel to every creature. It does not mean you will preach it to every frog that crosses the street, but you must be led by Him and His Spirit, meaning: "I am opening up salvation to every tribe, every tongue and every nation."

When you get in the Spirit, you may not pray for you and your kids, but it may be praying for somebody else. You may be doing all of this and that but never meet God's own need! You try to meet His needs while trying to do yours.

Those who do the things of the flesh mind the things of the flesh. They that are after the things of their own need mind the things of their own need. We are not of the flesh (need), but of the Spirit! When we are led by that, then we are the sons of God, not religious.

We are not debtors of the need or flesh because if we live after the need, we will always be in need. God knows what you need! Do you know what He needs? If you are always seeking your needs, you will never see what He needs. What He needs is what has the power. Let the Spirit reveal it to you and go after it! Submit to the Spirit concerning things that He is concerned about! The Lord is our shepherd. We shall not need or be moved by it but by the good shepherd!

The Spirit always moves us, leads us, and teaches us how to pray. He makes intercession for us and knows the mind of the Spirit. Be connected to Him, and you will know it as well! He satisfies us.

Father, I thank you that your Spirit will help us to walk after the Spirit and not after the need. We submit to your blood, power, and cross! No man, no religion, nobody can separate me or judge me, only you. We are the sons of God, and we will walk in the Spirit and not fulfill the lust, needs, or deeds of the flesh!

BREAKING BREAD

John 3, John 5, John 6:35-57, Romans 8

ANOTHER ANGLE

God woke me up morning. I know I have said so many things about this spirit in the past but here is what God gave me this morning about this spirit! Jezebel spirit will get you to go along with her plans — that is what empowers her. We must make sure that we do not ever empower that spirit because it will make you a eunuch. You start do what she wants not what God wants. All of a sudden, you are in deep.

The Jezebel spirit will cut you off spiritually and take all your strength in the Spirit! This is why she will run around and get people to agree with her plans, and if they are not God's plans, do not help, do not empower it! It will say God told me or showed me. Most believe it but many times, even their plans don't line up with scripture! It is very subtle but has its own agenda and undermines spiritual counsel and authority.

This spirit is very independent. It will seduce you with flattery and will make you feel very good and very important. You will be drawn to this person under its influence, but it's like a Mack truck coming out of nowhere. It will blindside you! You won't even know what hit you! The only way to help a person be delivered from it is don't feed it or agree with it or tolerate it! She does not have friends. She has victims because she rolls solo! She will look for information and secrets. She will find your weakness and use it against you! The people she uses are very wounded and have been abused and misunderstood and rejected.

When you point out things to her, she will divert it to another subject or person or place. No one can teach her but she will teach herself. She learns but on her own terms!

Male or female subjects, it does not matter what gender you are. She will find a place in her victims. She will use the word love to solicit you to help her because she will gain your trust then she will bite you, whoever she catches in her web. The Bible says we sin when we tolerate this spirit so that is the answer for what to do. That is not love? Did Ahab love her? In his own manipulated and controlled mind. Those who have ears to hear what Spirit is saying will hear! God bless.

PERILOUS TIMES

We are in perilous times. Look at the muzzle they are putting on the ox. Find your tribe before you get caught in a whirlwind. The Bible says that the beast will take over all seven mountains. We must flee Babylon. One is media: Now they are turning truth into a lie and lies into their corrupted liberal truth. This has never been an attack on freedom. The devil loves false freedom. It's an ATTACK on God, to stop the Gospel and the Bride! Hopefully, you can see it. This is why these doctrines of devils ARE trying to come in the church to seduce you to walk with the beast. It needs to be exposed. Where are we in the book of prophecy? False love is its biggest tool to deceive you. There are churches so carnal and the humanitarianism spirit brings confusion when only you have known the lamb, but if you have never encountered or spent time with the lion, you cannot know God fully. Come out from among them! Let God prepare you to stand on that evil day. WAKE UP, CHURCH! Your little paid conferences on your little movements of self-help are a waste of time. It's time to GET REAL!! The music is playing. It's time to dance! When real prophets and apostles are cut off on social media, how will you know where you're going? You must know HIM NOW!! WAKE UP!! Those who have ears to hear!

"Our fathers did eat manna in the desert; as it is written, He gave them bread from heaven to eat."

Luke 6:31

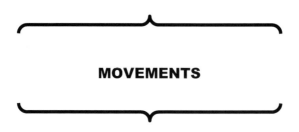

MOVEMENTS

So many movements in the body, but those that are man's movements move the body by winds of doctrines by man. The Word of God is the same yesterday, today, and forever. We don't need a movement. We need revelation from Christ always and every day.

One of these modern movements is the HEBREW ROOTS movement. It's anti-New Testament and a stumbling block to Christ. When people cannot tap into power and revelation, they become religious and try to tap into information. That does not bring transformation, just haughtiness in puffed up knowledge. It's not what we know that brings the Kingdom. It's being in one accord with HIM.

Before there were any roots, there was Christ, even before the foundation of the world. Don't let these religious letter carriers put stumbling blocks in front of you and deliver you leavened bread.

You cannot go any deeper than deep. Deep cries out to deep. The roots go to the deepest place. Why focus on a root when you have the creator and the foundation is Christ that every thing came out of. We were there before the creation in Christ. Stop worshiping what God created, like Jews, like man. Jesus said, **"And think not to say within yourselves, We have Abraham to our father: for I say unto you, that God is able of these stones** to raise up children unto Abraham" (Matthew 3:9). Worship Him where we live and breathe and have our being.

Converted Gentiles, trade in your tallit for a handkerchief and cry out for HIM. Jesus said Israel was a plan to bring the big plan: the Church, the living body of Christ. Do not look to a root! Be rooted in Him.

Know Him, not all about Him!!

WOW!

"That their hearts might be comforted, being knit together in love, and unto all riches of the full assurance of understanding, to the acknowledgement of the mystery of God, and of the Father, and of Christ; In whom are hid all the treasures of wisdom and knowledge. And this I say, lest any man should beguile you with enticing words. For though I be absent in the flesh, yet am I with you in the spirit, joying and beholding your order, and the stedfastness of your faith in Christ. As ye have therefore received Christ Jesus the Lord, so walk ye in him: Rooted and built up in him, and stablished in the faith, as ye have been taught, abounding therein with thanksgiving. Beware lest any man spoil you through philosophy and vain deceit, after the tradition of men, after the rudiments of the world, and not after Christ. For in him dwelleth all the fulness of the Godhead bodily." Colossians 2:2-9

COME ON!!

"For this cause I bow my knees unto the Father of our Lord Jesus Christ, Of whom the whole family in heaven and earth is named, That he would grant you, according to the riches of his glory, to be strengthened with might by his Spirit in the inner man; That Christ may dwell in your hearts by faith; that ye, being **rooted and grounded in love."** Ephesians **3:14-17**

Repent, for the kingdom of God is at hand. Stop letting religious demons take your identity in Christ and start to focus on transformation and revelation and the power of the cross. Don't look where He walked. Walk in Him now!

{

POVERTY SPIRIT

God has been showing me that so many are bound by a poverty spirit, and this spirit is always waiting for when they have more, then they will give. "When I get a big breakthrough then it will be different." The poverty spirit comes in agreement with the religious spirit, and it is in alignment with the entitlement spirit! Judas had it -- that is why he had an issue with money. He used the poor as a front to what he really wanted which was what actually belonged to God. So when he was with Jesus, He began to covet what he thought should be for the poor but was for the body of Christ, calling blessing a waste, not being led by the Spirit but by the need. Jesus said this need will always be. People who have a poverty spirit also have an entitlement spirit. They think because of the position they are in, everyone owes them in the church. It's church people in the church. In the world, it's the government. So they are never able to get ahead because they are always waiting. It is set in their mind to always be waiting to receive from God, but the Bible says blessed are those who give, not receive, so to break this spirit, we need to follow the Word! The only time we can't give is when we have nothing. This spirit always has a little, but it's measuring itself to others; in that, being entangled by the deception of its own cast system in the Kingdom of God. So instead of having eyes on the body of Christ and rejoicing in the blessing by the Spirit, they will have eyes on the money and judging the use of it in their own religious mindset, shutting down the Kingdom in their own mind and lives, saying if I had it, I would sow it, but God says if you are not faithful in a tiny bit, you will never be faithful in much. God is no respecter of persons. So let's get our eyes off one another and put them on Him where every good and perfect thing comes from above.

AWAKENING THE GIANTS

In the Old Testament, there were giants in the land, but right now, we are the giants in the land! Jesus came and gave us power over everything. We are supposed to be the giants in the land and to stop darkness! We are supposed to be the signs and wonders to a lost world. What we have, what we are doing, and how we are doing it, is important to God. It has to be what He is doing and how He is doing it. God has called us to do it His way! This is a wake-up call to all the giants in the land! Don't live back in religiosity! If you bring someone to the kingdom, and you become the living tract, the living Word of God, His oracle, then you really brought them in. Time to stop passing out tracts and to be the living epistle that we were all created to be.

Everything that I am telling you is in the Word of God, but if I have to wait for you to see it, what kind of messenger am I? If you have the kingdom of God inside of you, you will be very confident about it.

If you become a tract, they will hunt you down. What do we have to do to be saved? People think they will go to heaven because of their works. They are never born again.

In religion, you fall asleep but not under the anointing. But when you are hungry, the anointing will pull you in and out of time. For the religious people, they are like, "When can we get a cup of coffee?" "What's for lunch?" "Give me some donuts." This is a fasting by the Holy Spirit: You are so hungry for heavenly bread that you forget to eat. God will never give revival to a religious system. God does not move by needs. Everybody needs food, but people die hungry. Everybody needs salvation, but people will perish.

He is saying to us all: "I am calling you to do it My way. Not the way of your culture or your traditions. Doing it My way, this year, you will see the harvest, but you better seek my way, Peter." Peter got in the boat again and went back to the same old vomit even after walking with Jesus for over three years. Don't think you won't fall back without the fire and faith in His Word. Our traditions are not working and denominational ordinances are not working. He had to give it another shot. Peter decided to stop striving and do it His way.

The nets started breaking! The harvest was so much! And they went to the boats next to him asking for help! But now everybody is doing it this way and that way, but there is only one way to do it! It is called Jesus! When he saw the harvest, he fell down at the feet of Jesus: What kind of power is this? Peter said: Depart from me. I am so religious! Depart from me, God. I know my traditions separated me from God. I am so tired! I am so ashamed of myself! Peter really humbled himself! A church without the Spirit is not the church! Without the power of the Holy Spirit, we are naked just like Peter!

Before your eyes were open, you could never see your shame! Jesus met Peter doing the same thing He called him out of! The same place Jesus called Peter from he went back to that same familiar place. The comfortable place! And Peter was naked! Embarrassed! He denied Him three times! Peter, feed my sheep, my lambs! Peter was converted and never went back again! We have to follow Holy Spirit, not religion, not tradition, not denomination, but HIM.

We need to be converted! We need to repent and let God do church His way! We need to be a church where the gates of hell shall not prevail. That is the church of Jesus Christ! We have a godly form, a form of religion with no power! A church that walks in holiness has authority over the kingdom of darkness! A pure apostolic church! Repent and go back to Christ Jesus' ways There is a harvest on the other side! This is the end-time church that God is restoring. Awake! Awake! Wake up!

WHAT IS A WARRIOR?

Many men and women claim to be a warrior for God, but He showed me this (and I don't think we grasp it fully): we think that if we just love God, we are a warrior. But...

➢ A warrior never takes any offenses in their heart.
➢ A warrior lays down its right to be right.
➢ A warrior never gives up on its call or its assignment.
➢ A warrior is teachable and reachable.
➢ A warrior never complains about its assignment.
➢ A warrior's first cause is its cause and will not let anything come and distract them from its purpose and mission.
➢ A warrior will fight for love and never gives up.
➢ A warrior will not take record of wrong.
➢ A warrior will not put itself above others.
➢ A warrior does not count the cost. They just pay the price.
➢ A warrior's mission is to serve and not be served.
➢ A warrior does things to be seen of the one they are fighting for, not man.

- A warrior understands they may die, but they give their life for the cause.
- A warrior never jumps to conclusions. They weigh a matter, and they bring it before others and are slow to speak.
- A warrior guards its heart as it knows that it is what the entire war is about.
- A warrior will point you right to the cross, not to reasoning.
- A warrior will cast down everything that opposes love.
- A warrior will fight for the unity of the Spirit.
- A warrior picks up its cross every day.
- A warrior forsakes all for one they are committed to.
- A warrior does not gossip, backbite, or try to do things their way.
- A warrior does not entangle himself in the affairs of this life.

Are you really a warrior? Become one today. "*God, make me a real warrior for your kingdom. Help me to crucify everything that would make me want to give up or give in. Strengthen my hands for battle. Make me a living sacrifice solely acceptable to you. Change my heart and give me yours. Give me endurance to run this race without wavering. Make me an authentic warrior bride.*"

"Then understood they how that he bade not beware of the leaven of bread, but of the doctrine of the Pharisees and of the Sadducees."

Matthew 16:12

LEAVEN OF THE PHARISEES

Pharisees are people who are critical, judgmental, and faultfinding. They point their fingers at people, but they themselves do the same. The leaven of the Pharisees is hypocrisy. They are religious folks.

Hypocrites can discern a lot of things, but they can't discern things concerning the Body of Christ. They can discern nothing concerning the Spirit. Jesus said to them: "You can discern the sky and the weather, but you cannot discern this time," the prophecy being fulfilled right in front of them: Jesus! It is the same with the anointing. It is the same with the power of God. It is the same with the Spirit of God, but today Pharisees wear different clothes but they are still among us.

Hypocrisy is the leaven in everything that the religious people said. They look righteous, using the Word of the Bible, but they are living in unrighteousness! They miss right judgment, mercy, grace, and truth. They are worried about everything else but miss all of that. The most important thing is the heart, focusing on your little thing while they have lots of bigger things going on.

We are supposed to judge spiritually, to discern and test spirits but not judge by the flesh. This is up to God! The Pharisees did not judge rightly at all. They look clean from the outside but inside they are filthy. They are white sepulchers. Jesus did not let the Pharisees influence Him. Walking corpses knowing the letter and walking with the Word are two different things.

They find that little speck and judge you for everything. Scribes, Pharisees, and hypocrites are full of self-righteousness. Pride blinded them. They think everyone else needs to repent but them, that they are the only ones right. They are so high that they can't see Christ because He is so meek, lowly, and awesome.

Everybody would be like the worse sinner without Jesus. When you have that leaven in you, you thank God for not being like them! They ignore the power of the cross. All goodness about them was gained by dead works, by their own efforts, and by their own sects.

People full of the leaven of the Pharisees – hypocrisy – better stop judging because God will judge them. Our righteousness is still as filthy rags without Jesus.

Here is a great example: Someone will see some people smoking cigarettes then they say to them, "If you don't stop right now that is going to kill you. You will go to hell. You should be ashamed." Then they spew the tobacco out of their own mouths because, in their own eyes, smoking tobacco is way worse than chewing it!

Pharisees and Sadducees are hard to reach because they think they have arrived. They think they are holy but only in Christ are we able to be perfected.

When the woman was caught in sin, they only saw her sin because they were right in their own eyes. But Jesus called them out. They, one by one, had a moment of clarity concerning their own filthiness. They left, dropping their rocks. That conviction touched them. They wanted to judge her to death because of the letter, but through Jesus she found redemption. He told her: "Go and sin no more." But you see they did not repent. Religious people don't repent. They keep looking to accuse the righteous. The minute the woman was forgiven, she became righteous.

We should not judge any man after the flesh because you will become self-righteousness. Jesus' judgment is right. The religious spirit is antichrist, and the more Christ you have in you, the more they will hate you, persecute you, and revile you! They will say all manner of evil against you for His sake.

If you come against the Truth, there is no righteousness in you. Who killed all the prophets? The ones full of leaven! Jeremiah, Ezekiel, John the Baptist...they killed all the set apart people, but they themselves are all dead, dead men in a dead system. That leaven killed them all! Their leaven killed the Son of Righteousness. Surely, they will receive the Son of God? No. They said, "Let's kill Him and share the inheritance." So, who is in you? They hate the Holy Spirit. They said: "So let's kill with the spirit of Cain" (the spirit of murder).

Except your righteousness exceeds the righteousness of the religious people, you shall not enter the kingdom of heaven! Our righteousness has to exceed theirs because they have none. Theirs is filthy rags! The only righteousness we can find is in Him! We can't deny the power of the cross! Or we will strain at a gnat and swallow the camel. They can't even see it, but we have the chance to see it now!

God will show us His righteousness if we are hungry for it. This is the white garments we need to put on: Christ! When we are hungry for it, He will fill us with it!

Some of us put ourselves in prison because we are ignoring the righteousness that comes from Christ. You keep trying to exceed the righteousness of the Pharisees. There is no way to do it without Him!

Give us strong discernment concerning self-righteousness, Father. Cleanse us! We surrender for trying to get any righteousness without you. In that, we are as filthy as the scribes, Pharisees, and Sadducees. But in Christ, abide in love, truth, grace, and mercy. We are clean. "God, we desire clean hands and a pure heart," and the only way to have it is to abide in Him.

BREAKING BREAD

Luke 12, Matthew 23, Matthew 7, John 8, Matthew 5

EXPOSING HERESIES

Grace is the heavenly endowment to be able to do all that we could not do without Him. In the flesh, we cannot please God! Grace gives us the power over sin and death in that we work out our salvation with fear and trembling. There are many aspects of God's grace. There is grace unto salvation, a free gift that cannot be earned by human effort but only by faith in believing.

Then there is grace unto sanctification. This is enduring the fire of God and submitting to Him and His Word as we walk in the Spirit. He is changing us from faith to faith and glory to glory! Then in Jude is where men will turn the grace of God into lasciviousness and in that being turned over to a reprobate mind. This IS where people rest on the saving grace only and that is not the full gospel. This is heresy because it is without relationship and scripture is proven. God says to some, "Depart from me you who pretended to know me but I never knew you." He says if you love me, you obey me. The word of God removes the word of the world. We need to yield our entire being unto the power of God. When Jesus says to take up your cross and follow Him, this takes lots of Grace!!! False Grace or Hyper-Grace theology loves the cross that Jesus picked up, but they will not pick up their own. In this, they never become a living sacrifice but eventually fall away because they do not become one with the full counsel of God! So, heresy is preaching only His Cross when He preached two crosses: yours and HIS!

Not just ABC: You need R for repentance. Then add O for obey; then add F for follow. This telling people to say a prayer and your sins are forgiven is only half-truth because we must be converted and born again. Too many are being told that they are saved by an altar call or a prayer. I believe that saved people are different and the holy seed takes over and change happens. No matter where you are in the process, the key is you with Him in the process of relationship and restoration. Let's PREACH the full Gospel and don't deceive people. Only they can say they are saved. If you do not allow your mind to be renewed, you never understand that which is spiritual, and to be carnal is to be at enmity with God! He is Holy, so we must allow Him to be formed in us! This takes lots of surrender and Grace!!!

{

Many don't understand the deep things of God because they are charismatic prophets with worldly mindsets. NOW false prophets get it fast and easy in the religious system we call church. That's the easy way to sell books and CDs on how great you are now and can be. They entangle themselves in the affairs of this life. It becomes hard to see the bigger picture. Then they get offended at you, because you think differently and you really don't agree with them. The difference is that you're not living for now, and you are trying to get your mind off vapors and put it onto the eternal. So you will be misunderstood and people will think you are against what they say just because you see into the Spirit. That gets so frustrating! Imagine how Jesus rolled. I so love the progress of this nation. I am very excited in my flesh, but I cannot put my trust in man or their kingdoms. But I rejoice that my name is written in Heaven. There is a day coming when the bride of Christ will not have a nation or a leader. All they will have is Jesus. Give us eyes to see.

THE JOY OF YOUR SALVATION

God wants His joy to be strengthening us. His joy is the portion that comes with our salvation. God called the Kingdom of God Himself. We need the joy of the Lord. That joy is a well that you can tap into anytime. If you are living in depression, you need to be free. Most of us get in the way of God, and we live in bondage, never tasting His joy.

There is a counterfeit joy. There is a false joy, people acting up and acting out of control. There is no holy joy if you are not holy. It's only in Christ.

In Nehemiah, it was said: "Let the joy of the Lord be your strength," and through the outpouring of the Holy Spirit that joy can remain. Jesus is your salvation. If you don't have joy, you better get it back. That is no way to live, in heaviness all the time. He said, "Come all who are heavy laden and find rest."

People are so thirsty because they are not drinking. They are drinking bitterness, doubt, offense, and unbelief. You can be in the middle of persecution and still find joy! You will cry, but joy will come in the morning because He is our comforter.

We should be crying out to find salvation. In finding salvation, we will find joy. The soul shall rejoice in His salvation and be connected to Him. He will restore the joy of our salvation. David cried out for the presence of the Lord. In His presence, He found the fullness. David had a revelation of Jesus before He even came on earth in the flesh! He said, "Lord, bring me the joy of my salvation."

Our strength is Jesus! Without Him we can do nothing, but we still do a lot without Him. However, all we do does not bear fruit, and if there are any fruits, they won't remain unless we keep His Word! A good sign of false joy versus real joy: abiding in His Word!

If He is the spring of life, pump the well. If He is the spring of joy, pump the well. If He is the spring of strength, pump the well.

His joy will become your joy if you abide in Him by abiding in His Word!

If you stick to Him, living water will spring up out of you, but only if you abide. Selfish people can't have joy because they are only connected to themselves. Some people are so close to God, but they don't bear any fruits. It does not make sense, right? We need to have fruits of repentance. That is a sign of abiding in Him because when they don't do what He told them to do, they repent and go right back to that place of abiding.

We are all ORDAINED to bear fruits and fruits that remain! Do you want to be ordained? He already did it right here (**John 15:15**). Where are your fruits?

We are to have joy, the fullness of it! This is our portion. Why are we allowing ourselves to steal it? The devil comes to steal, kill, and to destroy your harvest of fruits.

Some people only want the benefits of salvation. There is no authentic joy without abiding in His Word. It won't last. The well of salvation is the fullness of joy! It is so tangible. The rebel dwells in the dry land. They can't ever drink from that well.

In the fruits that come from Him, there are no thorns and thistles. The religious people have learned how to live without water. They are like cactuses and palm trees. No roots. No water. And no fruits!

We are supposed to be oaks of righteousness. So, some people just get a little water here and there but not enough. Some people keep saying, "Look at the fruits!" They are all smiles but no real fruits at all! They carry not the fruit that comes from the real holy branch: Jesus!

The antichrist spirit will NEVER bear the fruits of the Spirit. It will never carry the real joy within. Then they will deny the real fruit.

Joy is the fruit of the Spirit. If you are not filled with the Spirit, you are not filled with His real joy. If you are not obeying the Word, you are not abiding in Him. Then your joy won't last.

Fear will cut off your fruit. Fear will cut off your faith. To tap into the well of joy, you need to have faith. Sometimes, because of the counterfeit joy, people get afraid to tap into it. False joy is out there, but real joy is available as well. Don't let the little foxes cut off your joy. Joy is your portion!

When His joy shall be revealed, we will be glad with exceeding joy! The Kingdom of God is righteousness, peace, and joy in the Holy Ghost. Broken cisterns cannot hold anything! Joy is not about people, places, and things. It is about Him!

Why do we need to keep testing the waters all the time? Either you know by the Spirit or you don't! Your spirit will discern it for you! I am not talking about Sunday's joy, when you walk in the room and have a smile on your face. I'm talking about that kind of joy that causes you to repent.

Joy is Jesus! He has become my salvation. Keep His Word. Abide in Him, and the fruit of joy will always be there. Your real fight is to stay in that place, not to get in that place because His blood already did it. It brought you to it! With joy, you can draw out more joy from the well of salvation!

Religious people say they love the Truth, but they don't drink from it! We can drink from Him, the well of joy, every, single day just by abiding in Him. No more garments of heaviness but of praise! Put Christ on, and dig into the well of joy!

BREAKING BREAD

Nehemiah 8, Luke 2, Psalm 16:11, Psalm 35:9, Psalm 105, John 15, Philippians 2:2, Colossians 1:11, Colossians 2:5, Isaiah 12

Simple revelation of the leaven of the Pharisees which is hypocrisy: Preaching and teaching the Word of God and not living it. This is why Jesus had so much power. He was living the WORD!

....

A sure sign to see who is in false grace and the false love movement (Apostasy): They will stick up for wolves and goats more than they will stick up for God and sheep!

DEMONIC DISTRACTIONS

God just showed me a vision. This is my prayer. God protect your doorkeepers and watchmen on the wall and throw Jezebel to the dogs. So I saw doorkeepers (true apostles) and watchmen on wall (true prophets) in position! Then I saw the Jezebel spirit in certain vessels. They were already in the city (church) inside. Then I saw some of them with the Bible trying to distract the gatekeepers with scripture out of context, cherry picking, emphasizing on love and taking scripture and turning it into spiritual fornication. They were dulling the swords of the anointed with their seductive worldly thinking that was void of the cross and using divination and witchcraft so other Jezebels could sneak in. Then I saw that because the watchmen on the wall were looking out and watching out for the sheep, some of them were being attacked from behind and pulled off the wall by their shirts. The Jezebel spirit was gathering Christians that it wanted. Also, these fornicating teachings sacrificed to their idols of lust, perversion, greed, self-seeking, and covertness were causing great division and blaming the gatekeepers and watchmen for bringing division. Apostle and prophets keep working together. Apostles keep building no matter what comes against them. You stay focused on your assignment as God, little by little, cleans the house of all the spots and the wrinkles! He is with you, for you, and in you. If that be so, then what can be against you!

"They began to relate their experiences on the road and how He was recognized by them in the breaking of the bread."

....

Luke 24:35

BREAKING MINDSETS & RELEASING STRONGHOLDS

Mindsets are formed from experiences. They are thought processes that will stunt your growth. The enemy does not have a stronghold. You are the one holding it strongly and not letting it go. Strongholds are set up for protection because when we are young and innocent, we have been hurt, abused, and taken advantage of, but Jesus says, "In the kingdom, we must become like a little child again," without reservations.

Children that grow up in the church have a lot of strongholds. They have believed a lie for so many years because of traditions and religion and denominational doctrines. Now they need the hammer – the right one – that will break everything that is not of Him! Sometimes you resist the right people and the right word in your life. You keep setting up your own boxes and fortresses in your mind. Only people that are set free can help others to be free.

Just like frugality, if you are frugal with yourself there is no way to be extravagant with others. We can be trapped in our own way of thinking. But let this mind be in you: THE MIND OF CHRIST! God wants to break our paradigm.

Who the Son sets free is free indeed. Are you really free indeed? Because we have been given freedom, let's walk in it.

Jesus broke the religious Jewish mindsets. Their traditions were not evil or bad, but they kept themselves from really knowing Him. The renewing has to happen by knowing the Word of God! It is impossible to know God without knowing the Word. By revelation, you can bring the kingdom.

God cannot live inside us fully until He can get past our strongholds. This mind must be in you as it is in Christ Jesus. Meditate on this! Act upon this! Not upon formulas and traditions. He does not want us to be bound by the way we think! Formulas can be good, but when they become traditions, they are not good. God is not an ABC God. He is faith and He is power. His grace is greater than our mindsets and our ways.

Our mindsets and traditions are strongholds. They cause us to expect something that will never happen because we are following carnality. We cannot think earthly because He is from above.

The church in Corinth was very carnal and worldly. They had worldly strongholds. Paul was telling them: take every thought of yours captive! The enemy wants to take up space in your mind! Through our strongholds, we are giving the devil permission if you are not letting the Word of God change your thinking. You hold onto something that was good but that will never take you where you are supposed to be. God is not a step program.

We break strongholds through obeying Christ and His Word. This is the exchange. I was a bastard, now I am a son! I was living a lie, now I am in the Truth. The Word of God keeps breaking the mindsets that we have planted from this corrupt world. God's Word with revelation will uproot every tree we have planted in our minds and break mindsets that have been put in there by lies.

You can't be something unless you think like it. So as a man thinks, so He is! That is why Jesus always says, "Let this mind be in you." The same mind that is in Him.

Little sayings can trap you! Then the enemy has your whole mind, and then there is a stronghold being formed. We have two hands. One has to be letting go all the time, and the other has to be receiving all the time. We are receiving from the Father as our mindsets are being broken. We are letting go of lies, like to be kingdom minded is to be no earthly good. This is another lie: this is just the way we are supposed to be. No, we are to be totally kingdom minded! We are not supposed to stay the same!

Renewing is to return! Don't relapse into your old thinking! Give up your will and your way of thinking, and let God renew it! The stronger your will is, the stronger your stronghold is!

You can't ever change the tree without plucking out the roots. You live in this prison in your own mind! God wants to give us His mind. That is what we are supposed to have from the beginning! This is not a one-time session that will fix everything, but a lifestyle! You can bury it or hide it, but you will never be really free because of your mindset! The Holy Spirit promises to guide us into all Truth, but we need to follow it. That is how faith works!

The Gospel of Jesus Christ is not the Gospel only unto salvation, but the Gospel of the Kingdom! We need to get hold of the Truth! Or you will become a prisoner of your own imagination, shutting up the Kingdom.

A spiritual man knows everything that the Spirit reveals to them! Their minds have been changed and renewed by revelation. They live from revelation to revelation and by faith, and that is what justifies them.

People with worldly mindsets always miss the heart of the Father in the matter! People go to hell because Satan shaped their mindsets. Their strongholds became their destruction. God turns

Christians over to a reprobate mind when they resist the Truth and don't allow themselves to change, saying things like: "I am never going to trust anybody again!" But breaking mindsets causes you to say, "God, I will trust who you trust." People with strongholds keep trying to find shortcuts but there are none! They have to lay down everything, and bring everything under submission to the Truth! They don't even trust the Holy Spirit. Their hearts become hard, and they call themselves wise, but God sends them the foolish things and people to confound them, foolish to the world but wise to God. His ways are higher than man's ways.

People do not like to retain God in their knowledge. They want the cross for Jesus, but they don't want it for themselves. "I am not picking it up," they say when they reject the Truth. They hold onto anything that exalts itself above the Word of God – which is Truth. This is false grace: They receive Jesus' cross but never pick up theirs.

An unrenewed mind and a reprobate mind – that is what they have. Because of our renewed minds, there is no old man anymore! You can try to have self-control in the flesh, but self-control comes from the fruits of the Spirit! See...religion wants to do everything by the flesh. Paul said we might as well go back to the law.

Paul was saying to the Corinthian church, "You are living with a carnal mind. You must have it renewed!" Their minds were exalting themselves above the mind of Christ. The Word of God is the mind of Christ.

By the Spirit and by His power, our minds are being renewed if we let it! The grace of God is changing us! God is saying, "Let it go," and, "Let this mind be in you." You are so strong, you are your own strongman, your own worst enemy! God resists the strong. He gives grace to the weak.

Some people have set their minds even about how they hear God. There was a season when God was using dreams to talk to them, but now God is using brothers and sisters. Their mindsets don't let them understand the mind of Christ! His ways are not our ways, but that stronghold will keep us bound by our ways! Your mind becomes stuck. Your conscience becomes seared!

Every time God reveals Himself to us, we are getting more freedom! Put on the mind of Christ! To think on things above (the Word), you need to be under it (submission). The devil will only flee if you are not double-minded! The only way to defeat the devil is by submitting to God and His Word.

If you have strongholds holding your back, it means you have pride because you won't let go. Get it right now! Some people go to the throne of grace with pride but not boldly. You will get no grace in that case. He only gives grace to the humble! He resists the proud. There will be no transformation when there is no renewing of the mind! Nothing is going to happen. The only way for Him to do anything in your life is by submission! He is not a tyrant king. He gives us a choice.

His thoughts are sober. Let your thoughts be sober, also! Remember: Stephen said, "Stiff-necked and rebellious. You always resist the Holy Spirit." We must submit to God, to the Body, and to the Word.

Sanctification happens by the washing of the water of the Word. You, as His bride, submit yourself to Him, as your bridegroom (as the Word)! Let every thought that does not line up to the Word be cast down, casting down imaginations and every thought, emotion, every teaching or tradition that exalts itself. Your mind is renewed by submission.

For this cause, we should leave the mind of this world, of carnality, and join to the mind of Christ, your mind becoming one with the mind of Christ! Leave mindsets and strongholds that are always exalting themselves! We need to be brainwashed by the washing of the water of His Word! The breaking of strongholds is done by the hammer of the Word of God. This is why it is a constant thing. Jesus is saying, "Let these sayings sink down into your ears."

Resist everything, put it in prison, everything that is trying to go above His ways and Words. Let His Words sink down in you, and let it be flesh in you! You can get the right mind faster if you humble yourself under His mighty hand, and His Word will lift you up.

God is not coming back for division or reprobate minds, but for people under One Spirit, One Word, with One Mind. People get so angry at the Truth but those people never change. Let this not be you. Let the hammer knock down everything that exalts itself above God. In the end, what needs to prevail is One MIND, and it has to be the mind of Christ and no other!

BREAKING BREAD

2 Corinthians 10:1-6, Romans 8:6-8, Romans 1, 1 Corinthians 2, Ephesians 4, James 4, Ephesians 5, Luke 9:44-48

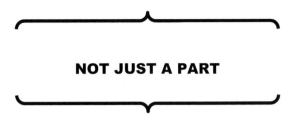

NOT JUST A PART

Religion wants to add Jesus into their life. Here is the far-left bordering on legalism, observing feasts that the Jews did. Jesus is our feast. Paul talked about grafting in but also talked about NEW creation! He spoke about our freedom. God showed me a lot! If you are a Christian and are observing feasts, you are religious, trying to add Jesus in. On the far left is the pagan Christ and false Jesus who is powerless; on the far right, we have powerless Pharisees and Sad-to-sees (Sadducees). Both are missing the narrow way in Christ. An unbiblical feast is what it is!!! The biblical feast to those who cry Abba father is to eat His flesh and drink his blood, 365 days, 52 weeks, and 12 months a year. Do not be as them, ever seeing but never perceiving.

In this message, I will go to extreme ends for you to know that there is no other way to please Him! We are now the tabernacle of God! So, in this, we lay it all down every day knowing that this is the only way to produce life! The difference between the kingdom of God and religion is that one becomes a part of our life and the other is our life. Organized religion says, "Let's bring Jesus into all aspects of our lives." The kingdom of God is, "Take over my life." God doesn't want us to add Him into everything, but He wants to be everything. The Holy Spirit guides us into all Truth and all freedom. Religion is always trying to do things in the flesh by rituals and methods, trying to make us spiritual, but the only thing that can make us spiritual is to die. By the power of God, He is making us grow into the full stature of Christ. There is nothing more spiritual than that.

Either you choose the resurrection and the life or you choose religion and death. The Kingdom of God is not by observation. You don't observe the feasts. You become one with all of Him and all the feasts. There is one new man, not in Judaism, not in religion, but in Christ. Heavenly Identity trumps any identity after the fall of man. The final plan was not Israel but the bride of Christ. Religious people keep adding seven feasts in their lives when Jesus is already IT. Everything points to Jesus. And now He is in us! They are trying to look more spiritual by knowledge, but God said they are babies bringing confusion and witchcraft. Seven is the number of completion in Christ. We fulfill all things in Christ. God is blowing our minds by His revelation, not by religious information, but the blind live off it. They keep eating from both trees and stay double minded and cannot receive anything from above because of their own strongholds and mindsets.

Why do you keep seeking information when revelation has already come to the World? Let Him subdue you! When you go back to what He said is decayed, you are crucifying Him all over again. Why are we observing the sacrifice of bulls and goats when God sent His own Lamb to be once and for all our atonement? The church is in an infant stage by the winds of doctrines and by the cunning of man creeping in and bringing the free back into bondage. They are so full of pride that they cannot even see the shame of their nakedness.

Jesus preached the Gospel of the Kingdom. Paul rebuked them sharply for preaching any other gospel. They take Paul's words of grafted in the olive tree and make their own doctrine around a tree that was created. We are not just grafted into a group of people or a system or a nation. Now we are grafted back into the Godhead itself. God is not pleased with you wanting to put this on His children.

Read **Ephesians chapter four**. Let that sink in. We are growing into the full stature of Christ, not into traditions, religion, and Jewish customs. We are co-heirs with Christ.

God does not want us to go back into bondage. People observe days, months, and times of the year when He is observing something totally different. Paul warned about those who put witchcraft on you and make you move in the flesh and steal your freedom in Christ. This leaven in their teaching is dividing His church. God says, "They will die with the letter." They ask and have not. They struggle in every area from finances to relationships and are cultish. It is the doctrines of man that divide the Body of Christ.

This word came from a dream. In this dream, there is a girl. She said, "I took out the highlights in my hair." Then I saw her going to the pulpit and taking my notes from the anointed words of God and the preaching. So, God showed me seducing spirits in this girl, taking, stealing the words of freedom, changing them into her twisted philosophy, taking out revelation and Truth from the Holy Spirit and adding her own religious twist and spin. So, in **Ephesians 4**, it says, "Until we all come to the knowledge of Christ." God is cutting off these lone wolves and all that add to His Word. - They have no power, no money, and no anointing. They have only their own interpretation of the scripture. Then they begin to yoke with the world and marketplace seduction to finance their destruction.

Paul, more than any Rabbi in this World now, could teach all of us about the feasts, but He chose to preach the Gospel of Jesus Christ and Christ crucified, to pick up your cross and to die! These feasts are heresy teaching. Anything that brings us away from Christ, not to Him, is demonic. The knowing all about a shadow or becoming one with the head of the church is totally different. They choose the ashes over the beauty and choose the crumbs over the feast. God told me to come harder than you ever have against this stumbling block.

Paul's biggest concern was to see Christ being formed in them. Are we sons of the bondwoman or of the free woman? You can't be both. Cast out the bondwoman! Cast out Jezebel! Cast out the religion! Cast out traditions! Get deep revelation about what really matters. For example, the whole book of Revelation is about the revealing of Christ and His bride. Religion made it a book of destruction. The children of the Spirit see demons, know people's hearts, and cannot be defiled. They test the spirits all the time and will not be deceived because they are from God and full of humility and grace. Religious zealots look humble, but it's false humility.

You can't be knit together with Christ and His body if you are observing what He is not. Rudiments of the world, enticing words, and knowledge that puffs up, this is all rubbish! We are free, not to do whatever we want to do, but to die to the world, to self-will, and to everything that the flesh wants.

The only thing that is holy is what comes from inside of Him. What is born of the flesh is flesh! Let's bless a mess? No. He does not bless a mess. He transforms everything. You want to add Jesus into your religion. Jesus is my religion!

How do you grow His church? Preach the Gospel. Eat His flesh. Drink His blood. There is no way to win souls if we don't do it His ways. So many do not want to walk with Jesus or do it His ways because you may have to die. Be the living sacrifice.

We are not adding Jesus into our life. We are asking Him to take over our lives. This is when things get harder: "Where should I go? The problem is only He has the Words of life!" We don't preach blessing. We preach the Gospel. It is the blessing! People are ashamed of Jesus and the cross, but don't let them get you!

I know Christians that would die for a country but would not die for Jesus. There is no nation that is really for the Gospel as a head at this time. They all belong to the beast. Only one is chosen! We are now a minority in the beast system and we are called by the Gospel to come out of the world. If we don't come out, we are in rebellion, and rebellion is as a sin of witchcraft.

Question yourself: Why are they all observing the feasts? Do they have the fire? Maybe they are not part of the same faith! Paul was more concerned about seeing us come into the unity of the faith and of the knowledge (not of the feasts or observances) of the Son of God.

Religion wants to bring Jesus into what they are doing. It is always trying to do things in the flesh, rituals, and methods, trying to make us spiritual, but the only thing that can make us spiritual is to die, allowing all the feasts (Him) to become our lives.

We are called to be led by the Spirit of God: One Spirit. One baptism. One faith. People are dying and on the way to hell. Christians are trying to fit leaven in the bread and the Body with leavened doctrines. We are called to preach the kingdom of God.

Let no man judge you in respect to observing the holy day!!! Do you really want to observe the seven feasts? Look unto Jesus! All every one of them points to is HIM!

- Passover: He is the lamb.
  The one who takes away the sins once and for all.
- Unleavened bread: He is the bread from heaven!
  Heavenly bread, not matza crackers that your fathers ate and died in the wilderness.
- First Fruits: He is the first among many!
  Of the born again, Jesus grafted us back where we cry Abba Father.
- Pentecost: The pouring out of the Spirit that never stops pouring out!
  He is in us, filling us now, and it will increase as we decrease.
- Trumpets: John the Baptist was one. The spirit of Elijah is one. You are one!
  Sound the alarm! Preach the day of the Lord is near. You are His shofar.
- Atonement: Jesus, His blood, is our atonement!
  We drink His blood daily. He is our trespass offering!
- Tabernacles: You are the temple of God not made by the hands of God!
  You carry His presence. You have God abiding in you 24/7.
  Done. You just observed all the feasts, looking unto the ONE, not just a part, not bringing Him into your religion, but because we are co-heirs and one with Him.

People are seeking for revival, but they are still holding back. Jesus bought us with His blood, and we do the same as Ananias and Sapphira did: We give him just a part of us. They gave a part of the land. "Why has Satan filled your heart?" You are always holding onto something. Why can't we give him all? He does not want you to observe His shadow. He wants you gone, taking over all of you. We need not lie to the Holy Spirit.

Many keep holding back to traditions and formulas, and God is saying, "GIVE ME ALL! Not just a part! Preach it ALL! Not just a part!" A lot of us lie to Him because we say, "God, take my life," and people don't really give it. All they want is to observe the dead when He is the living bread. Are you saving up your inheritance for the dead or for the living? Time to let the dead bury the dead!

Follow one feast: the biblical one, the whole Book in one. All 66 books speak about how He completes all things in Him. Come and eat His flesh, drink His blood. Feast on His revelation. See all provision. Don't just have a part. He died for all. God told me that when you observe the past you reject the future. When you do what the blind are still doing, you are coming in agreement with unbelievers that are still doing all the things that the first church did not do. Revelation is in you. God says that anyone looking back is not fit for the kingdom of God. All the feasts are in you. Rest in Him. Observe His ways, His Truths, and His power.

BREAKING BREAD

Galatians 4, Colossians 2, Leviticus 17:11, John 6:44-68, Luke 9:22-27, Luke 9:56-62, Acts 4:31-37, Acts 5:1-12, Ephesians 4:1-27, John 12:24-27

The amazing thing is that now we are the Word made flesh, the New Testament of His Blood, so we fulfill all things in Him! As we drink His blood and eat his flesh, as we walk in the Spirit, we fulfill all the fullness of God, being living epistles grafted back into the Godhead! What we could not do through the law, He did by shedding His blood, one time for all who will be transformed and surrendered, that we no longer sacrifice bulls and goats but ourselves. We no longer live by days, months, and holy days. Do not let anyone judge your freedom in Christ, but in Him we walk in His righteousness and in the Spirit as we are being changed from glory to glory, entering His rest from striving and the ordinances of man as He becomes our Sabbath, every day in His righteousness a holy, acceptable, perfect will of God from above. We now (man, # 6), as the 6 water pots being empty in the Old Testament, are now being filled in the new. What better way to give a demonstration in the natural than at a wedding? The first miracle at the wedding was representing man, empty, being made full, turning the water into wine, representing Him turning us into His image and filling us with new wine. We are the bride of Christ making a covenant in eternity.

We are being transformed into the image of the Creator. In Him, we breathe and we move in Christ, fulfilling all the law in Him. All who are in the kingdom of God are greater than Abraham, all the way to John the Baptist who Jesus claimed to be the greatest prophet ever. Now, as we carry this holy seed where we cry Abba Father, we now are born again from above, being partakers of the first fruits' offering of all who abide in Him. Anything or anyone living any other way is being robbed by religion and tradition and deceived by Jewish root idolatry and will never be transformed into the fullness of Christ. What cannot be done from the outside in, God is doing from the inside out, having now His throne on our hearts, producing life and godliness in our inward parts. The first testament had to be nailed to the cross. It was old and decayed. Now we have the New Testament of His blood and the law (word) written on our hearts, and the book of the law is in our bellies where the living water flows. We live as living epistles read by all men! We are living sacrifices on the holy altar as the grace of God gives us the power to be transformed and changed by the washing of the water of the Word that is renewing our minds.

In this covenant relationship, we are becoming free more and more every day! But the disobedient follow and worship the creation more than the Creator! God has a remnant that will not bow their knee to Baal, that are one with the Holy Spirit, walking in boldness as the grace of God purges them from all iniquity, not worshiping a dead letter but allowing the entire book to be lived inside of them. Any other creed or doctrine is from the father of lies himself and from the spirit of religion which is dead and will never produce life! Let this mind be in you that was also in Christ Jesus who thought it not robbery to be like His Daddy. God resists the proud and those who know all and are wise in their own eyes, who say they see but are blind. He gives revelation, grace, and power to those who choose to know nothing but HIM and Him crucified. Let us walk in Him and put on Christ, make no provision for the flesh and the law, and love as Christ loved and gave Himself for all. As you keep His commandments, He keeps you. What greater law than the one that all the ones are hanging on, LOVE! This is how we do it – The just shall live by faith in Christ!

"I speak not of you all: I know whom I have chosen: but that the scripture may be fulfilled, He that eateth bread with me hath lifted up his heel against me."

John 13:18

FREELY GIVING?

When a minister charges for a service that is supposed to be without money, this is not okay. It never was okay, but we have seducing spirits coming in the church! When a minister charges for his services, for even one thing, Jesus says, "Hireling!"

Remember this verse: **"Ho, every one that thirsteth, come ye to the waters, and he that hath no money; come ye, buy, and eat; yea, come, buy wine and milk without money and without price." Isaiah 55:1**

DEFINITION: hireling
~a person employed to undertake menial work.
~a person who works purely for material reward.

We are entitled to ask for an offering. That is the holy way. When we charge, we are making the Kingdom of God an industry just like the world and are prostituting gifts from heaven.

So, we are prostitutes. Sheep that give money for a service are Johns and the system of religion is pimping many out. God is not pleased with either of them. He threw both out of the temple. One bought and one sold. When you give money, you are coming in agreement with that spirit of Balaam. When charging, it means you are operating in the work of the Nicolaitans.

Here are reasons why a minister would charge:

- They are full of greed.
- They don't know any better and can't see full truth.
- They don't have faith that God is going to move and support them through the hands of man or open the windows of heaven.
- They consider their calling an occupation or a business, so in that, they are making merchandise out of God's inheritance. This is serious stuff, Beloved. The gifts and the calling are without repentance, meaning God will still use them, but they can lose Him.

KEY WORDS: GIFTS AND CALLINGS! You never see the people of God, the real leaders, put a price on fathering or teaching. The sheep will support willingly. We learn to hear God's voice in that as well! We want pure impartation!

- They trust more in the work of the flesh than trusting Abba to supply all their needs, as trusting in horses and chariots.

Fivefold ministry gifts are gifts to the body. Let's see what "gift" means.

DEFINITION: *gift*

~a thing given willingly to someone without payment; a present.

synonyms: present, handout, donation, offering, bestowal, bonus, award, endowment; tip, gratuity; largess; care package; goody bag; informal freebie, perk; formal benefaction.

So, if Jesus ascended on high, He gave gifts unto men. That minister is a GIFT to the body.

He also said what we freely receive, we must freely give. This is sin. It does not matter what is the end, even if it is for the poor, we need to do it God's way and follow the Word of God or the Kingdom. The ends never justify the means. We are either righteous or unrighteous.

God is raising up TRUE fathers, true apostles. They give all for their children and sons and daughters. God is pulling the cord on these merchandisers. He will have a church without spot or wrinkle! Let's pray for the brethren in error, but this has to stop. It's getting out of control. Jezebel is having a heyday. The Lord told me to rebuke it sharply. That is what Elijah does! I plead: Do not be a partaker of this cause. You will become part of the problem, not the solution. Selling prophecy and teaching is religion, not Kingdom! God is taking care of His true remnant very well! Let's pray that God raises up fathers, not hirelings, BUT shepherds and true fathers. Beloved, pray that they see and repent!

"I write not these things to shame you, but as my beloved sons I warn you. For though ye have ten thousand instructors in Christ, yet have ye not many fathers: for in Christ Jesus I have begotten you through the gospel. Wherefore I beseech you, be ye followers of me." 1 Corinthians 4:14-16

Before revival, there must be revealing! Pray as judgment starts in the house of God. If we care, we share. Silence is guilt by association. God is purging His bride. Pray for all who are entertaining this spirit. Please pray for me as I obey God! I'm like, "God, I don't want to do this." He said, "Who else will do it?"

You can be saying and showing one thing but people (believers) will see something entirely different. Make a remark and all you can do is shake your head. I said, "God, why does this happen so much?" He said that the carnal mind and the spiritual mind are at enmity with one another. Notice that some just get it and some just get you to EXPLAIN everything. We don't have time to explain God or His message. It's up to you to get in the Spirit. The only people Jesus explained things to were His disciples, but they did not have the Holy Spirit in them until the promise came. There are only few that find it, and let me add few that want it. He is explaining now only by the Spirit.

BLIND FAITH

The trial of your faith means you are being tried in what you believe. The trial of Joseph's faith took him to the palace. It was not an easy way. God is not in time. He has already seen in the future the things we are not seeing! The circumstances we are in now are what we begin to meditate and focus on. That's what brings worry and doubt. All the things we are going through around us works patience in us. God wants you to ask anything by faith. Reacting to circumstances to God is asking without faith. Not wavering is the only way to receive from God according to James.

This trying of our faith is worth so much more if we endure the trials. When we are tried, we receive the rewards of the Lord. Be content even in your trial. He wants to produce Christ in us. He wants to increase Himself in us so we don't have lack of anything. We must be single-minded and stable no matter what it looks like in a storm or in any situation.

We have to believe that He won't let us go to the left or to the right. The devil wants to steal that seed. Something does not look right, but we must believe He is still leading us. He is always there in the midst.

The promise came. That Promised Land is Him! The faith is what we should store up in heaven. From that faith, we will get our reward. The Word of God is directing us, just like all the things in the beginning when He spoke to us, giving us direction. We keep moving and keep having faith in Him!

Some people are sitting and waiting all the time, waiting for confirmation. All the time! Confirmation is not needed for those who are led by God and His Spirit. He confirms automatically. Whatever direction you move, right or left, you are being led by Him! Sometimes we need to go backward to go forward. Sometimes we need to decrease to increase. If your heart is not to make a mistake and to obey, He is our Father. He will make sure we are going in the right direction even if we make mistakes with a humble heart. He will turn us and it around. Under pressure, we need to stay on course. When pressure is on, the enemy comes in to try to bring doubt and unbelief. We must learn to shut the mouth of the adversary.

You must ask Him, knowing He loves you, and He will give you whatever you need to take you in the right direction. You say, "God, I don't know your will, but lead me," then you get up and move. The Father gets up to lead you. The enemy will try to bring confusion, telling you that you don't hear Him. Once you know Him, you know IT. Act on what you know and on what you believe. He is His Word, and He is faithful to complete that which He began.

We are kept by the fire of God. If you don't see it or feel it, we are still kept by His fire. Circumstances don't matter. Abraham had relationship with God and was kept by His fire. Faith is the currency of heaven that we deposit all the time! Without faith, we can't please God. Period! Faith does not look like anything that the carnal eyes can behold. You can't really see faith with carnal eyes. The only time you see faith is after it produces the substance that you were believing for. That's why it has works.

We need to flee from the temptation of going ahead of God as Abraham and Sarah did. God said, "I want to do it this way or go in this direction," but they looked at themselves. "We are getting old, we need to do something, or we won't inherit the promise. This is taking too long. We are getting older. Has God forgotten us?" Then we try to help God, and then we get into a mess when we try to do it in the flesh. We need to believe that God will move and do whatever He wants when and how He wants. This type of faith is unshakable and is the only type He wants.

The Word does not say, "All things work together easily," but "work together for HIS good pleasure." God wants to work with people that give Him pleasure, the foolish things of the world, the kind of people like us. These are the chosen ones! They don't have it all together so God gets the glory. Trust God when all the ducks are in a row and when they are all over the place. The fear of the Lord is faith. That will keep you. Fear of the world is a faith killer.

Blind faith! You may not know about tomorrow, but you still believe. Walk by faith not by sight. You are rich not because your bank account said so? No. Because you have God! You are healed because you don't have pain? No. Because His Word said so! Don't speak out of what you feel or see, but by the Word of God.

Abel believed God but never saw Him. He was found righteous because of his faith. Enoch walked with God – the invisible God became visible because of his righteousness and obedience. Blind faith shows itself when we walk in it! The evidence of your belief will speak at the end. When we believe God, works show it! The kingdom will expand in our lives. We need to trust Him. Speak His promises in any situation! Keep seeking diligently. This will show the evidence that you believe Him. When we walk in faith, we walk in obedience.

I don't see the rain, I don't see any clouds, but I believe it is going to rain because He said it. Ask Noah. Abraham kept walking and believing, and God led Him! Your Faith cannot be in what you see. Keep walking by faith! Man does not know the future. God does. Keep your faith on Him so He will prepare you for any storm! He knows the future. When He tells it to you, it's up to you to believe Him. That is where faith comes from, by hearing and believing Him. Abraham did not know where he was going, but He went. God wants to eliminate the little Ishmael that comes along the way. That is why He is leading us by His Spirit. You take that leap of faith because you heard Him! Keep speaking the vision, especially when it has not come to pass yet! That shows God your faith! That is why He said to speak those things that are not as though they are. Why, because to God it has already happened! He will increase us if our faith increases inside of us and if our faith is not in our own strength. We pray that our faith will be increased in every area. Faith in Him that we are saved. We will see in the natural what we believe in the supernatural. He is a God of truth and mercy. It is His good pleasure to give us His kingdom! Take it by faith!

BREAKING BREAD

Psalm 85:8-13, Psalm 37:21-32, 2 Corinthians 5:7, James 1:1-24, 1 Peter 1:3-9, Hebrews 11:1-40

WHAT IS IT WORTH?

What you value, you honor. What is given without price is considered without value in some mindsets.

For example, salvation was given freely. In this, some do not value it as if it were earned. But easy come, easy go. There is not the same value when you work hard to attain something. So, in our carnal mind, sometimes we devaluate it. That's what hyper-grace does as well. It devalues it when it cherry picks its own scripture and creates heresy. When we become a part of something, when we sow into something, when we labor for the thing, it becomes worth more to be a part of it. What is value to you because you were not the one paying the price for it? We devalue what He really did sometimes when we don't pick up our cross, so we never really see and become one with Him. Because if all that people say is just believe in all that He did but never do our part as a relationship requires, we are receiving a doctrine of devils. We must see the value in what He did, the price to pay, so He wants us to partner with his sufferings, His rejection, and His being hated. This takes a full gospel. This takes enduring, so in the end, you have a lot of value invested. How are you going to keep it if it's so frivolous and does not have all your heart?

You can put your name on something, start something in the nations, or just give money and open charity works in nations, but they may not value it. Many lose the value on what Jesus did because they don't sow into it, no labor for the right value. Have you ever heard "easy come, easy go"? Like if you are working your whole life for something, it will be of more value than just winning the lottery. You may waste it in a fast manner.

If something is earned by me, I can give it more value. This is why we need a balance and a full gospel, all of Jesus parables, to understand this FREE gift so we don't lose it. But if someone just gives something to you, then you don't take care of it. In false grace, your heart can't value something because it is all about what He did without considering your need to do your part. In a covenant, in a marriage, it is a partnership. Unless you are a gold digger and you're just after one thing: not going to hell. But Jesus saves, not just saves us from hell but to destroy the works of darkness. Paul boasted on everything he went through for Jesus and not on everything that He did for Jesus. Add the right value on what is given to you: Your calling, your identity, your ministry, and so on, will not have value if you are not partaking in the cups that He drank.

Go purchase what He is giving to you through endurance. Pay the price of going through because this is the way you are showing Him what you value, what you go after. Do you really value TRUTH? If you do, you go after it. The more you see the value, the more you invest in it. Dead people do dead works. Nothing has eternal value for them because religious activities are not God's plan for us. It's not, "Do this and don't do that." It's partnering in the valuable things, like His heart, His pain, and His rejection.

If you get a false gospel, you can have false converts. You need the full Gospel to get full converts! People change the names of their congregation but never the foundation or the heart. They don't show any value for the right Gospel because they don't preach it! Have you counted the cost? Did you sit down and think about the cost of following Him? Then when you are really showing value, you are showing that you are really for Him.

For some, the Gospel of Jesus Christ is too much. They don't see the value of it. It is worth losing all. It is worth what Jesus said, forsaking all. Do you want to hear a man water down and devaluate our Master's plan? Let's talk about salvation. He saved us so we can become Him on Earth and destroy the works of darkness. God is saying, "I did not save you just because you need to be saved but because I have a plan here on Earth for you to do." People talk about Jesus but never tell them they need to die for His sake. They have relationship with themselves. Never did the Gospel of Jesus Christ say, "Easy come." Everything that He gives to you, you need to pay the price to keep it. Unless you don't value it, you will let it go easily.

You are never really going to see how great the investment is until you die! The Kingdom of God is the retirement plan for eternity. We are so more carnal that we are so worried about investing in a future on the earth and value our life now that we plan and live for it. This is not the Gospel. You invest now and you reap in eternity. If we really believe that Jesus is the One, we would never follow any other. It is time to walk this Gospel with value! How much is blood worth?

In **Matthew 25:14-36**, Jesus calls people that don't value what He gives, "a wicked person." They did nothing with what was put in their hands. That wicked servant never valued what was given to him so he lost it. The unprofitable servant was thrown in hell! That relationship between them never increased. He gave that talent to the servant and was expecting him to increase it, but he did nothing with it. What are we doing with what He did?

In **Mark 14**, the woman with the alabaster box valued Jesus so much that she poured everything, every drop of it, at His feet. What religion calls waste, Jesus calls value! People act so carnal because they don't see any value on the oil. You can do religious duties all the time, but can you really value Him?

People don't see the value in others that are full of oil, so they don't value Christ in others. They are devaluating what God is always validating. The religious people were putting more value on the poor than on Jesus.

Jesus is saying, "The things that have value are the things that I put value on," but religious people always will say, "It is a waste." They have no kingdom mind. Judas got mad and went back to the religious system, trying to get something from them, because in his eyes, he got nothing from Jesus. The religious system wants to steal and kill. Think of Judas! If we don't see the value in each other, we will become like Judas.

The woman did not even try to save the box. She broke the box. She did not try to save anything. She valued Jesus more than her possessions. Extravagant investment! There was nothing more important than Him. Are you going to be mad like Judas when you see somebody doing what you are not willing to do: To pour out all their value on Him? Don't call anything waste unless your eyes are able to see like Jesus sees.

In **Luke 7:36**, one of the Pharisees wanted Jesus to go to his house. Sometimes what bothers you is one specific part of the Gospel. What part really bothers you concerning the Gospel? The woman was weeping and crying, and they got mad at her. The oil went down His body. She wiped His feet. Then they questioned Jesus, "If you are really a prophet, you would know who this woman was." Now, they were not mad at the wasting but for receiving that woman. But they hated the woman because she valued Jesus more than her reputation. Their focus was on sin, not on mercy. She was already received because she valued her God. Will you value what He values: the least of these? In **John 12**, it says the oil was very costly, and for a burial you always need oil. But they forgot about what Jesus kept telling them was His purpose. All they thought about was the price.

He sees our value. We need to see and value Him back. When we value one another, He pours more value (His oil) in us. Because that means that we are ready to die! Let us be living and anointed for daily burial. Be the one that was never forgotten by Jesus! That woman was everywhere in the four Gospels, and God made sure to make her memorable because she put all her value on Jesus. She valued Him. Don't give for any other reason than only because you value Him. He has commanded you to love with all your heart, mind, and all that is within you. He paid it all! Are you buying the field? **"Again, the kingdom of heaven is like unto treasure hid in a field; the which when a man hath found, he hideth, and for joy thereof goeth and selleth all that he hath, and buyeth that field" (Matthew 13:44).** Are you just using the field to play and build your own identity? Are you valuing the treasure in darkness? What profit is it if you gain the whole world and all its false value and lose the treasure of life?

BREAKING BREAD

Mathew 25:14-36, Mark 14:1-10, Luke 7:36-40, John 12:1-11

"But let a man examine himself, and so let him eat of [that] bread, and drink of [that] cup."

1 Corinthians 11:28

THE ONE

Many are lost, but I tell you this. God is looking for you! He is looking for everyone that has been born in this world. There are two wills to be done, whether you know or not.

You will follow God's plan or Satan's plan. There are only two plans on the Earth. There are only two masters on Earth, whether you know it or not, but there is only one that you will bow down to in the end, so we bow now to the one and only true and living God; then we have an expected end. You will bow to God that creates heaven and earth now or at the end.

If you are bowing to any other god, the god of self or the god of this world, then you are bowing to Satan. It is better to follow the creator than the one who was created. Because hell was not made for man but for Satan himself, and whosoever follows him will end up where he ends up: It's called hell.

God is looking, and looking, and looking. As long as you have breath, God will keep looking for you. We don't know how much time we have left, but God knows. That is why the closer to hell you are, the harder He looks for you. When I was about to die, He was looking really hard for me. But until I rended my heart and said, "God, I can't take it anymore, I don't want to live my life like this anymore," then He came and found me. It was the fear of the Lord that graced me. I was lost, but He knew exactly where I was. He knows where you are.

When He found that lost sheep, the one, He put it on His shoulder and carried it on His shoulder. It is time for you to let God carry you. You have been running for a long time. You have been doing your own thing for a long time. Even some that already know Him started doing their own thing, and we become lost even after we have been found. Time to come home. Today can be your day to let the Shepherd carry you back home, to carry you all the way back home. Just let Him.

All heaven rejoices over that one that is found than the 99 that don't need repentance. You are that silver coin.

He is seeking for you diligently. You are His treasure, but you need to repent. You need to recognize that you are lost. He will come and find you. He loves you so much. You are His little sheep, of more value than silver or gold.

He paid the price of death for you. You must receive Him, believe Him, and repent. You must admit that you won't make it without Him. The only thing that stops us from being found is our pride. Pride kills but grace heals. God resists the proud but pours grace upon the humble.

After hearing the Gospel, the only thing that sends people to hell is not even sin but unbelief. That is the sin that is unforgivable if you die an unbeliever. Because everyone is able to be made whole, all who believe. God is no respecter of persons, so He is perfect. It is not just to believe how good He is and that He has paid the price for you. You must believe in Him, pick up your cross, and follow Him. If you are tired of trying to be good, give up. The only goodness we have is in God.

God is drawing many to Him, and He says, "Come through my Son." He is the first voice and the last voice. Nobody knows when your last breath is. How many more days do you have to live? It is not going to be your sin that will send you to hell today after hearing the Gospel. It will be not receiving salvation for your sins and not receiving the Gospel of Jesus Christ after hearing it. Yes, because of not receiving, then all sins remain!

It does not matter if it is just ONE PERSON. We are after THE ONE that God is after. All heaven will rejoice over that one. Will you hear Him today? Will you be the one? Let heaven rejoice over you coming home today!

BREAKING BREAD
Luke 15:1-10

FOUNDED ON THE ROCK

Solid as a rock: this is how we have to be. The only way is to be built on the Rock. The Word is Christ, and He is the Rock.

"Why do you call me Lord, Lord, if you don't do what I say?" Many come to Jesus, but they do what they want with only the things He says that they like. We are all supposed to build but upon HIM! Not built with a bunch of stuff in between. He says: "Dig down and find that rock," but most of the time we have to keep digging between the mixture to find a little rock, which is not even Christ – the Word of God. To find the sure foundation, you must dig past man's ideas, theories, genealogies, and all the religious roots.

"Now therefore ye are no more strangers and foreigners, but fellow citizens with the saints, and of the household of God; And are built upon the foundation of the apostles and prophets, Jesus Christ himself being the chief corner stone." Ephesians 2:19-20

Lay the foundation upon the rock because the storm is coming. Before He splits the sky, there will be the biggest global storm the world has ever seen. We need to be ready and be on the Rock, or we will be shaken. You can go to the church, for instance, called "Cornerstone," but if it is not the real foundation, it is filled with man's ideas and dead works. There is no solid foundation. It will surely fall. If God is raising the volume of the voice of His messengers, there is a reason. The time is short!

The pastoral churches are not founded upon the Rock. We need to hear His sayings and do His sayings. We need to hear the Word that comes out of His mouth. This is why Jesus puts His messengers in position. The reason is that God is a God of order. He set the entire universe in order. By Him, all things were made that were made. Anything built on man's ideas or on denominations will fall.

A wise man builds his house upon the Word of God. A foolish man builds upon his own opinion. We cannot afford not to be upon the Rock! If you can't stand when little storms hit you, surely you won't be able to stand when the big storm hits the Earth.

You need to stand upon Him. Your identity is not on you, what you do or say, but in Christ. People are building churches upon worship, or prayer movements, or evangelism, personal prophecies or supernatural events, or works of justice. But none of that is the right foundation, but CHRIST in His fullness is. He is the foundation of HIS OWN CHURCH! All of these are to enhance the Word (the Rock), but the foundation must be sure.

We need to know the Word, and the Word needs to know us, or we will become like the Pharisees and Sadducees that ignored the foundation – the cornerstone. They identified themselves with a man but hated His words – the words of life. Religious people hate the same words of life today.

People buy land by what it looks like. It looks good from a carnal perspective. It has nice trees, pretty flowers, lots of space, and a great view. They bought it in the dry season, but then it began to rain a little rain, and it becomes swampland. During raining seasons, they will be in trouble because they built upon sand and mud. The foundation has to be way down deep. The foundation was there even before the beginning of time. Before day one was zero, that is where He started, Ground Zero, and that was what God created.

You never build in the middle. You start on the corner. If you don't start with Jesus, it won't work. He is the chief stone. The cornerstone! How can a church survive if He is not there? How will we survive if we are building on man's foundation?

God will not build anything upon man's foundation. He can't. He won't. The apostles get the blueprint of HOW TO DO IT. The church is built upon that foundation – the foundation of the apostle and prophets – because God gives them the plans straight from Himself. That's why man shuts down the authentic prophets and apostles because they are carnal, but you can discern the false. They lie to you, telling you that Paul was the last apostle. That is one of Satan's biggest lies. How can that be true if God said that in the last day there shall be false apostles? If there is false, there is also true. If Paul was the last apostle, why would God warn us to stay away from the false? (**Matthew 24:10-12**)

So God sets forerunners apart for the restoring of the broken down gates. A church without protection is a church without a solid foundation. It is like untempered mortar. Have you seen those hut houses or mud houses in Africa? Most houses (churches) are not tempered mortar, just dirt, wood, and stubble! Our souls can't hold it all together. The Holy Spirit has to. He is the one that holds it all together. A tempered mortar is hard; it is sound and strong. It is stuffed with the bonding in the cement that binds it all.

Apostles and prophets are in the business of building His church. Satan made many believe that they are all gone. Dead. In doing so, disorder entered in. But they are all over. God's plan never changed. The blueprint was given to these specific men to build the church on the Word.

If God has not called you to build anything, you do not have the right to build anything. Your passion, your titles, your ordination and certificates from theology school make you a fool if you move in the flesh and do not give you the right to do so. God wants us all to be back on the Rock. Let every man make sure that you build right and upon Him, Paul said.

So, what we have are building materials that are man-made and recycled, plastics, Styrofoam, and man-made materials. But God tells us what to use and how to use it, just like He told Noah exactly how to build the ark. Apostles are God's engineers. He (GOD) is the master builder. Many labor in vain.

People that are worship-centered should use worship to enhance the Rock (Word) and to get us back to the Rock. Worship helps us to stay on the Rock (Word). Prayer-focused helps us to get to hear Him and stay on the Rock. Evangelism is about getting people on the Rock. See? It is all about the Rock (the Word).

If any man builds upon gold, silver, precious stones, hay, or stubble – these all shall be manifested! People say, "That is not a big deal. That is just a little thing." But when you put all the "little" things and deals together then that becomes a "big" deal. No. We can't enjoy a man's foundation because the door will not be shut. The God of love told Noah, "When the door is shut, open it for nothing." It is important to preserve what God is building. God will make it clear and plain. He will expose this kind of foundation. He is exposing every other foundation. He is shaking all. If it is not on the rock, you will fall. That is why apostles and prophets pluck up and clear away the ground and all the dirt to lay a sure foundation. That is why they must be totally set apart. These mainstream apostolic networks today have so much mixture. They have never removed it, so they become false and unstable. Surely, they will fall.

Trust. Obey. Follow. These are simple instructions. If you live by Baal, you will die by him. If you live by the sword, you will die by the sword. If you build a wrong foundation, you will be crushed by it because it will fall. Jesus is a serious preacher.

Don't let any man deceive you with their wrong foundations. Let the fire burn. Let Him crush anything that was not built by Him. Lose your life now, or you will lose it later. Satan is into legalism. He will use the Word of God to condemn you all the time or to "help" you build something with the wrong foundation. He is the prosecutor. He will come after you even if you decide to obey His blueprint. He will turn on you, using your wrong ideas and man's interpretations, and he will condemn you with the same Word that should give you life.

Moses went to the rock to get the water! Go to the rock, and I will put water in it! Go back to that rock: CHRIST! That is where your living water comes from: The Word (Rock).

If you are not on the rock, what makes you different from people that ran the temple back then? Any difference? No. Whoever despises that rock is saying to Jesus: "Shut up, Jesus, we got this." Paul, the apostle, called Jesus the builder and the cornerstone. He got revelation straight from Him. Peter did the same. Don't build anything upon any man's revelation but upon the revelation given by Him. This is why Jesus says fall on the rock (**Matthew 21:44**), build on the rock, or be crushed by the rock. If you don't build on the rock (Word), you will be condemned by the Word and crushed by the Word. We must live by His sword. Let His sword kill all man's agendas.

There was a foundation even before any foundation. In the beginning, there was the foundation: The Word. Jesus spoke it, and it was created! The foundation for His church was ready even before anything else. We can't know Him without knowing the Word because He is the Word. How can you love somebody without knowing that person? The same happens with the Word. If you get mad at the Word, you don't love the Word, you don't love Him. Take heed of the leaven that is put in the bread. Take heed of the mixture that is put on the foundation. Take heed of what they added to the Word. When it was time for Jesus to go, Peter was not saying the word of God back to the Word of God. He did not want Jesus to be crucified, but that was his carnality. "Get behind me, Satan." But Peter later went back to the foundation. He was stable and solid as well. If we don't know the Word, we cannot speak the Word to the Word, and anything that comes out of our mouths will fall to the ground and produce nothing.

If you have been with the Word of God long enough, you would have known what Jesus really looks like and how the foundation should be. If any other thing is in the way, you must remove it.

Peter is called Cephas – the rock - but he is not the one we build upon. Upon the revelation of who Christ is: that is the right revelation. We build on the revelation of the Word only. Anything built upon a man is a harlot. Anything built upon Jesus is the church, the Bride. Only those who are built upon the right foundation, whatsoever they loose is loosed in heaven; whatsoever they bind, it is bound in heaven. To only those, the keys of the Kingdom were given. To only those, the door of hell will not prevail. These apostolic keys of authority are only for those who live on the rock – a fastened and sure foundation. Let us allow God and His apostles and prophets to remove all that is between you and the Rock!

**"And whosoever shall fall on this stone shall be broken: but on whomsoever it shall fall, it will grind him to powder."
Matthews 21:44**

BREAKING BREAD

John 1:1-17, Luke 6:43-49, Ephesians 2:19-22, Matthew 7:20-29, Romans 15:19-22, 1 Corinthians 3:9-23, Psalm 118:20-29, 1 Peter:19-21, Matthew 16

{

The Lord will answer any one of us according to the multitude of our idols. Many have of us have strangled ourselves from Him through our idols. Idolatry is adultery. We spend most of the time fornicating with ourselves. It is spiritual masturbation. It is all about us or our idols. We go to bed thinking on ourselves, or on them. We wake up with all of our idols in our bed. And we go to someone to inquire of Him wondering why He is so far from us? The Lord Himself will answer us by Himself and will expose to us how we, a house of prayer, became a house of idolatry.

The foundation is set. It is firm. But the walls are falling. Look at all the pictures of our lovers hanging on the wall! We have set up many idols in our hearts. We have put our own stumbling block of our own iniquity before God. We have separated ourselves from Him. He won't compete. "Adulterers shall not enter into His kingdom...". He will let us go farther and farther until we repent. We have provoked His anger. "Thou shall not commit adultery." We have provoked His wrath. "Why doesn't He get closer?" Why, do we ask?

Like a camel that goes through the eye of a needle, shall be again our relationship with Him. In the beginning was Him and us. May today be like it was in the beginning, and may it remain like it was in the beginning all the way unto the end.

Marlene Roessiger

"And they continued steadfastly in the apostles' doctrine and fellowship, and in breaking of bread, and in prayers."

Acts 2:42

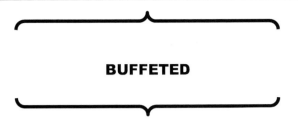

BUFFETED

Paul was speaking about being buffeted by a messenger of Satan because of the abundance of revelation. **"And lest I should be exalted above measure through the abundance of the revelations, there was given to me a thorn in the flesh, the messenger of Satan to buffet me, lest I should be exalted above measure," 2 Corinthians 12:7.** There was a thorn in his flesh because of all the revelation he was getting, and he said in his own words, "That thorn was a distraction, a hindrance, a nagging or irritating in the flesh." Have you ever had a thorn?

What is a thorn? Small or big, you can't get it out right away because you need the right tools, so usually, it is there for a while. Paul was trying to dig it out by bombarding heaven. A thorn is not something life-threatening. It can't kill you but irritates you. It is constant. God wants to desensitize us from the things that agitate our flesh and use them to remind us we are nothing without Him.

Buffeting is a continuous assault, to afflict, to lash, to harass, to torment, or to trouble for a very long time. Was the thorn – the messenger of Satan – possibly a hindering spirit? I believe so. According to as much information Paul had given, it seems that God was using Satan for his own purpose to keep Paul grounded and humble.

Sometimes we, through sin, invite Satan to mess with us, and that will also humble us, but if we don't have that thorn in the flesh, we won't have the need for Christ. Without the hand of God, we will become full of pride as many in religion and the world do, so we rejoice in His chastening. Sometimes that thorn in the flesh is just to remind you that you are human. Just because you are "working with God" does not mean that He will fix everything in your life. Whatever goes on in our lives, we still need to look to Him. What God decided to do, He will do it. Keep your eyes on Him and never on your circumstances. God knows what to leave in us and what to take out. Sometimes pride makes us believe that we deserve something from Him, forgetting that the only thing we deserve is really hell outside of the cross. God gave Paul deep revelation about the bride and He did not give it to anybody else. Lest he would be exalted, God kept him low through all of these infirmities (meaning afflictions) that the power of God would rest on him.

His weakness kept Him focused on Jesus. On His infirmity (which is not even just sickness), Paul boasted. Because He knew the power of Christ would rest upon him. He may leave something on your flesh so His power can be manifested. Paul did not die on the road to Damascus, but he kept dying daily. He kept his flesh under submission to God and to the cross. If we observe through the scriptures, we can see through his writings how much Paul became humble as he walked with Christ.

Sometimes, we are doing things that are inviting Satan to come over. When we live in sin, Satan can come and touch us. That is not the buffeting of God. That is you being beaten up by your own ungodly choices. If you keep walking in the flesh, you will die by your flesh. Lustful flesh! This will kill you. He will torment you. He will beat you up, like Paul turned one over to Satan to destroy his flesh but to revive his spirit (**1 Corinthians**

5:5-7). So, God will use even His enemies to correct those whom He loves.

How do you know if you are being buffeted by God or beaten up by Satan?

Check your righteousness level, meaning are you walking in the Spirit or the flesh? Are you walking in holiness, in His way? It's His holiness. We must be submitted to Him.

Don't bend to your flesh, but if you bend to it, go boldly to the throne of grace. Bold because you know what He did for you. You can know everything about the power and never tap in. You can know everything about the cross and never pick it up. You can know everything about submission and never submit. You hear all about grace but don't use it in righteousness.

By the abundance of revelation, Paul was buffeted. If the buffeting stops, that is a sign that the revelation stops.

The buffeting is to take you away from your flesh, not away from God. It is to draw you to Him and to see His power rest upon you.

Anything that comes from God is to bring you to the cross and His power.

When we sin, we know it. But when you are in righteousness, you also know. There is a difference between to like to be around darkness or to be sent to darkness. Be aware of it.

You can be in His presence and still be buffeted, exactly because you are in His presence. For the abundance of revelation, glory, and presence! So you will remember to stay low!

All things He works together for good for those who love Him. He never leaves you or forsakes you. Make sure you remember that when you are being buffeted! God wants to keep and to preserve you! The enemy loves to lie, to bring up the past, and to accuse you. So keep your eyes on Him.

"Guide me Holy Spirit. Deliver me from every evil work. Sustain me. Raise me up. Make me walk in truth all the days of my life. I cast off ungodliness, every lie from the devil. I confess the blood of Jesus over my mind, heart, will, and emotions. My flesh will not rule me. My mind won't trip me up. My tongue will speak good things. In that, I submit my whole spirit. Jesus, open my eyes and let me see the path you have set before me that I may walk with you all the days of my life."

"Father, if it is needed, keep buffeting me because I don't want to be separated from you because of the abundance of revelation, Glory, understanding, power, and presence!"

BREAKING BREAD
2 Corinthians 12:1-12, 1 Peter 2, 1 John 5:18, Romans 8

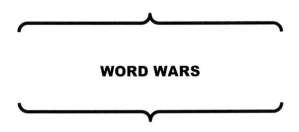

WORD WARS

We know there are two kingdoms: the kingdom of darkness and the kingdom of light. There are two heavenly hosts: the fallen angels and God's angels. There is a constant nonstop warfare in the heavenlies, and there is a word war down here on Earth.

God says that we, as believers, are the ground control. We have authority with our words. So we need to line up our words with the Word of God, and then we will put to flight our destiny. We must not allow our tongue to work against ourselves. We say a wrong word and then Satan, the legalist that he is, will use that word to work against us.

So we speak things that are not as though they are. Whether you feel it, or you don't. Whether you see it, or you don't. We can't submit to our feelings or to the natural. We need to speak against it. The enemy has the mouth of many shut, but God is opening them up now so we can use the sword of the Spirit and put God's heavenly host to work for us, not against us.

We will tell them what to do. No negative agreement over here and there because the angels of darkness will carry those words on as well. If we don't like what we see, don't speak it. Speak life and light! Our words of life will overcome the enemy's words. Watch what you speak! Angels (of light or darkness) have power if we give it to them because we have authority if we are a child of God. Whatever you speak on Earth will be done in heaven.

God works and moves by His Word. If we don't speak it, nothing will happen. Put the right thought in it! Take out what the enemy says, and put in what God says. We need to stop letting the devil use our tongues. Maturity has to do with how we control our tongues.

The Word will stop anything. Obey the Word, and everything else will be lined up. Walk in the Spirit, and you will speak spiritual things. The problem is that we end up going back to the basic things – the milk of the Word – all the time and never get to the maturity we are supposed to. We stay carnal. We need to go back to the Spirit. The spirit man is a free man!

The Word of God has to be our foundation. Satan turns our thoughts into our words, and once we start speaking, we put darkness in power! So many people say whatever and don't know why they stay in their mess. Single-minded people are always stable. The Word penetrates our minds, and we start speaking in agreement with what we believe. This is why we take captive every word and thought and whatever comes in our imagination that does not line up with God's Words. If we don't, we will begin to speak for the devil and not for God.

Speak things that are in the Word. It does not matter what you see or feel. There is nowhere to run but to the Word of God. There was only one church for them back in the book of Acts time for them to run to. They learned to change the situations by believing, praying, and enduring all things in love. They had to deal with things with the Word of God. They could not leave the church because there was no other church. They were the only one in the city. They were not denominational but family orientated, not organized religion, nor did they have planes or cars for them to run away. There was only ONE church in their region.

So still today, there is no other. Fight for your brother and sister with the Word of God. Believe what it says. There was never a Plan B in the Bible or in the book of Acts. Look at the power manifested when we are fully committed to one another and the Word of God.

The enemy plants in you things you want. The flesh fights the death on the cross, but you need to learn to pick up your cross. You don't get promoted because you have been in a long battle but because you pick up your cross. The devil is legalistic. He even uses the Word of God for his own gain. He can and will use it against you. Think of Jesus in the desert being tempted with the very Word of God. The Word of God was being used against Him. If Jesus had allowed His situation or His natural man to lead Him, He would have fallen. But Jesus said the Word back to Satan: "It is written."

When I am not in a good place, I have to be in a quiet place. I need to not be around people who are in a bad place. Run for your life, or you will be speaking bad words and cursing with your own mouth. If you curse, you will live under the curse. Endure the chastising. Live by every Word that comes out His mouth, not your mouth. By your own words, you can bind yourself. "I will never do this and that." Don't speak out of your emotions.

Satan messes with our communication. He wants us to say whatever we feel or see. But love says the Word and takes no record of wrong. Satan kills, steals, or destroys. We need to break these inner vows because we speak those things out of emotion or frustration. God told you to do something but the outcome was not good, then you start giving up. You start wavering. You start to be put to sleep. Then when we feel tired of standing and fighting for the Truth, we began to speak out of the abundance of how our heart feels. If you have evil in your heart, you will speak evil. If you are unstable, you will speak life one day and another day death. We should protect the words. Don't ignore the person, but protect your words. Take one step back, and make sure that the next time you speak, words of life will come out of your mouth. We are commanded to love our enemies and to bless those that curse us and to pray for those who misuse and mistreat us and not to speak badly about them.

Let us be abundantly filled with the Word of God, abundantly filled with love, and abundantly filled with peace. Don't tell the enemy what he wants you to say. Your flesh wants you to do this and that. Your flesh hates the cross, and when it is time for you to pick it up, your flesh will try to stop you just as Peter did to Jesus, but you need to say, "Get behind me. I will go to the cross!" The greatest enemy of the cross is not Satan but your flesh, your own will. This is a form of rebellion. This is why it is very important to be a hearer of the real Gospel and do it.

Be founded on the Word. Don't be built on your circumstances or your environment or on what you see or feel. God has put us together. He knows what He is doing. You will be tossed to and fro if the Word of God is not your foundation.

When you get your tongue under submission, your whole body will be saved. James talks about that: the man that bridles his own tongue. Just like we put a bit in the horse's mouth, we need to allow the Holy Spirit to tame our tongue and to train it in how to speak.

Your tongue is little but powerful. It is the tongue that defiles your whole body and defiles relationships. God uses the example of a ship. Look how big the ship is but then look at how small is the rudder. It controls the entire direction of the huge ship, so shall our tongue. A person that is not submitted to the cross or Holy Spirit cannot control his tongue. Nobody can contain the tongue. If you are not submitted to the Holy Spirit, you will never be able to contain your tongue. It will start fires everywhere and will burn up all the good! We must learn to control it. James says that you will be tossed by waves and end up where your circumstance wants to take you and not where the Word of God wants to take you.

When we use authority in a wrong way, we will bring hell upon ourselves. Out of the same mouth cannot proceed blessings and curses! This is not how it ought to be. Bitter and sweet waters? God's fountain brings forth only living water! We need to use our mouth to advance the Kingdom of God inside and all around us through our mouths! We will either bring life or death!

Our main purpose is to die! Stop agreeing with what you have inside you and bend to the Truth and you will be speaking life! Don't speak what your flesh wants. "I, I, I," but God is saying, "The Word, The Word, The Word!" There is only one "I" that needs to prevail, the great "I AM", not you, not me, but HIM! Let Him prevail in your mind and mouth. God is saying, "There is no way to reach you if I cannot teach you."

Your mouth will bring you to confusion, heresies, strife, and envies. You had better be quiet rather than lying against the Word if it is not submitted to the Word of God. When we cannot keep our emotions in check, the Body of Christ will help you to line it up. This is why we need people on the Rock around us.

We keep complaining with our mouth and asking God for other things than what He has given us, but we need to understand that all things work together for our own death. You can speak to the mountain to be removed, but if what you say it by the flesh and not by the Word, the mountain will stay right there. We all get tired of speaking what we don't see, but we need to go back to the sincere milk of the Word! Feelings or the Word? Flesh or Spirit? Natural or faith? Love never fails. Love never gives up. Love keeps no record of wrongs. See everything with the eyes of love, and you will be encouraged and empowered! Your tongue will speak life because your heart is full of it! Only out of the abundance of it you will speak!

Go to the cross. Rend your heart. Humble your tongue under His Word. The Word will bring you up. The Holy Spirit will lift you up. Get your lips back in alignment. Get your heart back in alignment. You can't stop halfway. You have to go all the way to the cross. Training is brutal. The fire is hot. But it is always worth it. Sin is to know what is right and not do it. What is right? The Word of God! Go to it. Do it. Death and life are in the power of what you speak. You will eat the fruit of it. If God said you are holy, and you don't feel it, you will think you are dirty, but that is just feelings. You can't blame anybody because you are the one going by your feelings. Go to the throne of grace, confident, and you will start seeing you clean again!

You will eat the fruit of what you believe and think. Don't speak anything contrary or Satan will move your direction because your tongue controls your whole body. This is a serious word. We will eat the fruit of our own words. Let it be good fruit.

Decree and declare the Word of God: I break every lie of the devil. I put the blood of Jesus over me. Align my whole being with your Spirit, God. I repent for speaking anything that was evil, doubt, or unbelief, from my emotions or feelings. I untie the knot.

I break apart every word that did not come forth from the Word of God. If I cursed myself or anybody, Jesus as the son of God gave us all authority and power over every evil. I call them back. I take the power of every word, every word that did not line up with what you say, God. I release blessing over my Church, my life, my wife, husband, family, children, and self. Satan, I command all of your words to fall to the ground. I am strong. I have a calling. I have a destiny. God has plans for my life. I will not be tossed to and fro by the winds of doctrine. I line myself up with His fresh living water. I speak it over my life, and I call back every single word, and I take all the power over the enemy's camp. I send forth all the angels in heaven that work for Jesus Christ to bring the finances, bring the healing, bring the cross, and push back the devil. I decree that I have the victory. I have lost a few battles, but I will win the war. Jesus is the author and finisher of my faith. It is not my emotion, not feeling. This is the war that I make through my word for me, and I release the blessings of God. We agree with every Word of God. Everything will come to pass. Help our tongues, Holy Spirit! Let us not lean on our own understanding, but lean on our husband, the Word!

BREAKING BREAD

1 Peter 2:2-4, John 10:10, 1 Corinthians 3:1, James 3, Luke 6:45-49, James 4

"Unleavened bread shall be eaten."

Ezekiel 45:21

MAN PLEASING VS. GOD PLEASING

One thing God is showing me about man pleasing and it's really deep because we turn ourselves into our own puppets. Man pleasing is rooted in pride. It's about you and being accepted, being liked, and being received.

But God always looks at the heart! That's why He hates man pleasing because the man you are trying to please is yourself!

Acceptance is a really deep well! Most times, you are already accepted 100%, and you just don't know it! This is a fine line. What really is the truth of the matter is that you are being nice for personal acceptance and gain or because of the cross. The big thing people do not understand is that it's all about the heart and very little about the man!

The thing is they say they are not going to do something because, "I'm not man pleasing any more!" That's not the issue. What you are doing is why you are doing it. That's what God wants to change. Because what you are doing is good. God says, "I want you to do it but do it for Me, not for you!" Deep calls.

God uses those things, our insecurities and our rejections to train us to do what we are doing. Now He wants us to do it in the Spirit and in Truth! But never what we have been doing has been the issue. It's been the why! God says now do it with the cross. The greater the love, the greater the cost. The greater the cost, the greater the loss. Lose your life to gain it. This baffles the world. It is so anti-world and so Christ that it just irritates even the thoughts of them who hate the cross.

God wants the root exchange, not the fruit exchange. What you do is for God, not for you! This is a form of pride! When we do things for our own reasons, it's just flat pride masquerading as one sold out to serve, love, and live for Christ. But those who see by the Spirit know the difference and smell it, see it, and just know it! The one "man pleasing" works to show their love. The person who is "God pleasing" loves, and we see it by their works as in the book of James. It's not what we are doing that needs to change. It's our hearts.

What happens is that some learn about man pleasing then try radically to change. God uses our selfish motives to please as a starting point then He turns it around to teach and turn it into a God pleasing motive. But without the cross, we can become religious and dead. On the contrary, we probably even do more when doing it in purity and in truth, just our initiatives change and the intentions are no longer personal but eternal. What we do is for the advancement of the kingdom and of one another, not our usual self. The fact of the matter is when you are not pleased with the man, you will stop your good works and deeds and serving and say in your heart, "I'm not doing this because I'm not pleasing man." When pleasing man is not pleasing to you because of your heart, it's really God you're not pleasing, and you are now in the flesh.

Then you shut down time and time again. This is where the rubber meets the road. We think we can outsmart God, but what He does is reveal to us and then we hide. Pride hides when God reveals the heart because that's what pride is about — you!

Love is about another. See, this is where we see what we do and stop doing what we are doing. Like being nice, having kind words, doing kind acts, serving, blessing, encouraging, giving, and loving righteously. Do we stop this? Of course not. We just do it unto the Lord and not unto you.

Man pleasers will not be steady in their walk because of pride! Let us do all for the Glory of God, not for the glory of man. Let us do to be seen of God and see the heart of man and love without any selfish motives. I tell you the truth, pleasing God is so pleasing to man, and if you learn to please God you will be the sweetest incense to both God and man. What you are looking for in your quest will be accomplished here in this age and in the age to come eternally true. Stop pulling your own strings, and let the cords of heaven move in His direction every time.

SPEAKING IN TONGUES

I did not realize what a conflicting topic this is so I added scripture right along with it. This is something you can just copy and paste and be done with it to any who are being deceived. Line upon line, exhaustive full-counsel. Enjoy. Long but worth it! Know how to give an answer when asked!

I come emphatically with a word of correction and warning from God. There are some that call speaking in tongues gibberish, some call it babble, and some are calling it tongues of devils! These are Christians that post scripture like crazy. They judge by the letter and not by the Spirit. In this, they take and change scripture for their own private interpretation. That is also wrong! They will say this: We must not judge by encounters but by the Word. Actually, the encounter must follow the Word if the Word is alive and real. You see, this spirit is so legalistic that it blinds them to their own interpretation, deceiving and shutting down faith for God to do what He wants to do. So this is true: I heard about speaking in tongues, so I asked God for it as a baby Christian. Then I was baptized in the Holy Spirit around a week later in my bedroom. So here is scripture!

"Ask, and it shall be given you; seek, and ye shall find; knock, and it shall be opened unto you: For every one that asketh receiveth; and he that seeketh findeth; and to him that knocketh it shall be opened. Or what man is there of you, whom if his son ask bread, will he give him a stone? Or if he ask a fish, will he give him a serpent? If ye then, being evil, know how to give good gifts unto your children, how much more shall your Father which is in heaven give good things to them that ask him?" Matthew 7:7-11

When I awoke I was speaking in an unknown language, not gibberish but to the natural man that might be what it sounded like. I was not a theologian. I was not a bible scholar. I was just a hungry baby, just born again a few weeks, seeking God with all that was within me. Now you are saying that I asked for the Holy Spirit and I got a serpent (devil)? Since that day, I have been praying in this language and being changed from glory to glory and from faith to faith. So in the book of Acts and every time they were filled with the Holy Spirit, they began to speak in tongues as a sign to unbelievers and evidence to them that they have it.

"And when the day of Pentecost was fully come, they were all with one accord in one place. And suddenly there came a sound from heaven as of a rushing mighty wind, and it filled all the house where they were sitting. And there appeared unto them cloven tongues like as of fire, and it sat upon each of them. And they were all filled with the Holy Ghost, and began to speak with other tongues, as the Spirit gave them utterance." Acts 2:1-4

They ALL spoke in tongues. So by truth and revelation, continue to read the rest of this passage. It says:

"Now when this was noised abroad, the multitude came together, and were confounded, because that every man heard them speak in his own language."

It did not say that they spoke in their languages but that they HEARD THEM IN THEIR OWN LANGUAGE as they were speaking in tongues. So if God makes you speak in tongues when you are in a different nation, they may hear it in their own language, and the Spirit is the one making the interpretation. But that is not its main reason like religion thinks: so people can hear the Gospel. No. That happened on that day. But God has His own heavenly language and its purpose is so much more than just that. Plus, He even says we can even interpret our own tongues through the gift of interpretation.

"And they were all amazed and marvelled, saying one to another, Behold, are not all these which speak Galilaeans? And how hear we every man in our own tongue, wherein we were born? Parthians, and Medes, and Elamites, and the dwellers in Mesopotamia, and in Judaea, and Cappadocia, in Pontus, and Asia, Phrygia, and Pamphylia, in Egypt, and in the parts of Libya about Cyrene, and strangers of Rome, Jews and proselytes, Cretes and Arabians, we do hear them speak in our tongues the wonderful works of God." Acts 2:6-11

There were 120 people speaking in tongues because they just got baptized. God was using that noise and translating it into their own languages, into each one's own differently. They heard about the wonderful works, not of the devil, but God.

Here is where they miss it and twist it: they said that they SPOKE in their language!! NO, the Word says that they HEARD them speaking their own language, meaning God through His miraculous self-made these people hear the unknown language in their own language. Is GOD not capable? If He can take your tongue, He can have your ear! There were many different nations and languages represented there. So, to the mockers and unbelievers, it sounded like gibberish or babble, but some heard it as being the wonderful works of God. Imagine 120 people speaking in tongues, all at once, and God doing that just so people could hear about Him. What was a sign of confusion, but to some that sound is very precious!

"And they were all amazed, and were in doubt, saying one to another, What meaneth this? Others mocking said, These men are full of new wine." Acts 2:12-13

The outpouring of the Spirit was a prophecy fulfilled, but He never stopped pouring it out. These other religious people are mocking even today. Some say it is "works of God," some say "works of the devil." Which one are you? The mocker? Or the believer?

So are you one that is amazed like I am and was with God and the Holy Spirit? Or are you one in doubt like mockers calling God's treasure from heaven and gifts a bunch of noise and gibberish, saying we are fools that speak and pray in unknown tongues?

Those that do this don't have the baptism of the Holy Spirit. That is the problem. How can you be such a scholar on something that you don't know? You know the letter and quote the letter, but does the letter know you?

Even Paul said that the letter kills and the Spirit brings life. In other words, the Spirit brings the written Word of God alive with the Holy Spirit revealing Christ and the mysteries so we can know all things He wants us to know. We have the gift of revelation and all the other gifts He gives at His will working together for the edifying of the body as well.

When they were filled with the Holy Spirit and with fire, they all spoke in tongues, as you see in the scriptures below. What you also need to take note of is this was way after the day of Pentecost and is still happening today as God never changes. Once He tore the veil, the Holy Spirit is on the earth doing the same ever since. They say they are Bereans but they get their knowledge from denominational doctrines and theologians void of His Spirit!

Today we have many claiming to be modern day Bereans, but without the Holy Spirit, they can keep searching and they will find nothing because they don't have the spirit that can translate and explain all things. We don't look for knowledge, but Him! I don't need to hear from doctors of the letter but from Him!

"That your faith should not stand in the wisdom of men, but in the power of God. Howbeit we speak wisdom among them that are perfect: yet not the wisdom of this world, nor of the princes of this world, that come to nought: But we speak the wisdom of God in a mystery, even the hidden wisdom, which God ordained before the world unto our glory." 1 Corinthians 2:5-7

You know what they say, "Oh, Brother, we don't go by experience," but I tell you this: "My experience is followed by the Word of God." Signs and wonders always follow the Word.

So let's look at other encounters:

"And they of the circumcision which believed were astonished, as many as came with Peter, because that on the Gentiles also was poured out the gift of the Holy Ghost. For they heard them speak with tongues, and magnify God. Then answered Peter, Can any man forbid water, that these should not be

baptized, which have received the Holy Ghost as well as we?"
Acts 10:45-47

They heard them, and they magnify God. Our tongues magnify God. Boom! They received the gift of the Holy Spirit even before the baptism of water. Didn't I say they knew what was being said in this passage?

"And it came to pass, that, while Apollos was at Corinth, Paul having passed through the upper coasts came to Ephesus: and finding certain disciples, He said unto them, Have ye received the Holy Ghost since ye believed? And they said unto him, We have not so much as heard whether there be any Holy Ghost. And he said unto them, Unto what then were ye baptized? And they said, Unto John's baptism. Then said Paul, John verily baptized with the baptism of repentance, saying unto the people, that they should believe on him which should come after him, that is, on Christ Jesus. When they heard this, they were baptized in the name of the Lord Jesus. And when Paul had laid his hands upon them, the Holy Ghost came on them; and they spake with tongues, and prophesied. And all the men were about twelve." Acts 19:1-7

Every one of those who were baptized with the Holy Spirit spoke in tongues! It is in the Word! So humble yourself, and you may receive it as well. We have all the things that God has given us: the letter and the Spirit.

The Word of God is alive to us. What happened to me when I received the gift of tongues still happens to me today. It never stops. That is the fruit of it. Don't call what is of God of the devil. Someone can end up in hell for that. So be aware of it. God will never hold anything back from those He loves. God may have a lot of mercy because you did not know before, but now you do! You better repent!

This passage in **Acts 19** talks about other disciples because the twelve had already received the Holy Spirit in the upper room. The first thing in the apostle's mind is: Do you have the Holy Spirit? But others will ask: "How many scriptures do you know?" You are the one bringing confusion, coming against those who know the Word of God. Imagine a new baby believer being baptized by God in the Holy Spirit and in fire. Then this one comes to you, and you say, "It is not real. It is demonic." Woe to you!

Peter preached, and as he was preaching, many received the Holy Spirit. Paul laid hands on them so they could receive it. God is still the same. God never changes. He is the same yesterday, today, and forever.

So above you see believers without the Holy Spirit's baptism. That's what we are dealing with today as well as their mindsets are stuck on what they have been told or been shown to see. But none of them speak in tongues, meaning they don't have the baptism. So the ones with the baptism are trying to show them and help them, but God resists the proud. The gift of the Holy Spirit will come in humility and grace only. This is how it looks in this parable: It's like you have been a fisherman all your life and you never went to school. You just did it and learned from trial and error. You have been catching fish like crazy, and you know what you are doing because you have lots of fish. Then this person comes with a book and tries to tell you that you are not a fisherman. They look and can't see in this book what fishing looks like, and they have no fish only a bunch of knowledge from some man that was a fisherman. You're thinking, "Yes, but I can't believe

I'm wrong because look at all these fish." This is what these people do when they come against those with the gift.

God says we are dead Christians without the gifts. The priest needed pomegranates representing fruit and bells representing gifts. If bells were not ringing, the priest was dead. We are all called priests now if we have the blood of Jesus and if we have been born again. Dead Christians continually quote dead words as well as posters of dead ministers denying the body that is alive around them, worshiping dead as if God is not speaking now through His gifts and through His Body. They get the spirits of Korah and Cain. They submit to nothing but their own understanding.

These people say that the gift of speaking of tongues has ceased. Let's see what the scripture in **1 Corinthians 12** says:

"Now concerning spiritual gifts, brethren, I would not have you ignorant. Ye know that ye were Gentiles, carried away unto these dumb idols, even as ye were led. Wherefore I give you to understand, that no man speaking by the Spirit of God calleth Jesus accursed: and that no man can say that Jesus is the Lord, but by the Holy Ghost. Now there are diversities of gifts, but the same Spirit. And there are differences of administrations, but the same Lord. And there are diversities of operations, but it is the same God which worketh all in all. But the manifestation of the Spirit is given to every man to profit withal. For to one is given by the Spirit the word of wisdom; to another the word of knowledge by the same Spirit; To another faith by the same Spirit; to another the gifts of healing by the same Spirit; To another the working of miracles; to another prophecy; to another discerning of spirits; to another divers kinds of tongues; to another the interpretation of tongues:"

Most believers still believe in the gift of healing but don't believe in the gift of tongues or interpretation of tongues. Is that not very interesting?

"But all these worketh that one and the selfsame Spirit, dividing to every man severally as he will. For as the body is one, and hath many members, and all the members of that one body, being many, are one body: so also is Christ. For by one Spirit are we all baptized into one body, whether we be Jews or Gentiles, whether we be bond or free; and have been all made to drink into one Spirit."

So now we don't drink from the same spirit because the apostles died? Very interesting. Times are worse now. God is coming back for a church without spot or wrinkle and full of power. So that was a concern to the church back then and not for now? Come on! It makes no sense.

"And God hath set some in the church, first apostles, secondarily prophets, thirdly teachers, after that miracles, then gifts of healings, helps, governments, diversities of tongues. Are all apostles? are all prophets? are all teachers? are all workers of miracles? Have all the gifts of healing? do all speak with tongues? do all interpret? But covet earnestly the best gifts: and yet shew I unto you a more excellent way."

Diversities of tongues! Do we all speak in tongues? Do we all interpret? We can, but we should ask. It is all available for sure if the Holy Spirit is still running the Church. Major denominations have poisoned the holy water with their doctrines of man and of the devil.

"Though I speak with the tongues of men and of angels, and have not charity, I am become as sounding brass, or a tinkling

cymbal. And though I have the gift of prophecy, and understand all mysteries, and all knowledge; and though I have all faith, so that I could remove mountains, and have not charity, I am nothing." 1 Corinthians 13:1-5

Everybody believes in the fruits of the Holy Spirit but deny His power (the gifts). They reject its heavenly language. So below you see all the gifts from above, but man has dismantled the Bible. Paul said if any man preaches any other Gospel, let him be accursed!

The gifts:
- **Romans 12:6-8**: Prophecy, Serving, Teaching, Exhortation, Giving, Leadership, Mercy
- **1 Corinthians 12:8-10**: Word of wisdom, Word of knowledge, Faith, Gifts of healings, Miracles, Prophecy, Distinguishing between spirits, Tongues, Interpretation of tongues,
- **1 Corinthians 12:28**: Apostle, Prophet, Teacher, Miracles, Kinds of healings, Helps, Administration, Tongues
- **Ephesians 4:11**: Apostle, Prophet, Evangelist, Pastor, Teacher

So we don't have the word of knowledge anymore, they say, but Satan does and that is why the palm reader has them, but God's people don't? So Satan's handmaids get more than God's? Doctrine of devils saying that the end time church does not have power anymore! How come? He said the glory of the second house shall be greater! We are the witnesses! We are the martyrs! The end time church has power!!! I have news for you: If you don't have power, repent!

Let's read **1 Corinthians 14**:

"Follow after charity, and desire spiritual gifts, but rather that ye may prophesy. For he that speaketh in an unknown tongue."

He did not say foreign language but unknown tongue.

"...speaketh not unto men, but unto God: for no man understandeth him; howbeit in the spirit he speaketh mysteries. But he that prophesieth speaketh unto men to edification, and exhortation, and comfort.He that speaketh in an unknown tongue edifieth himself; but he that prophesieth edifieth the church."

Paul is saying, "Use your gift of tongues to not only edify yourself but do it to edify the whole Body." He is saying: "You are speaking unto God, not unto man." So, of course, Satan wants to stop us from communicating with God!

"I would that ye all spake with tongues but rather that ye prophesied: for greater is he that prophesieth than he that speaketh with tongues, except he interpret, that the church may receive edifying."

Paul did not say, "You have to have someone to interpret." If there is no interpreter, then be aware of the surroundings so you don't look crazy. He is not saying, "Don't do it," but you can be speaking in tongues just to edify yourself. If we interpret what the Spirit is saying that will edify the Body. When we pray in tongues, we are speaking and praying ahead tomorrow. Sorry to say but those who don't have the gift are jealous of those who have it. Spirit of Cain. This also is in the book of Jude. You begin to hate your own brother because of your heart. God said concerning Cain and Abel: "If you do well, God will receive you!"

"Now, brethren, if I come unto you speaking with tongues, what shall I profit you, except I shall speak to you either by revelation, or by knowledge, or by prophesying, or by doctrine?"

People quote this scripture, but there is no revelation. If there is someone who is speaking in tongues, some religious people may be confused, but I am not speaking to them. I am speaking unto God. According to the scriptures, I am in order, but to them, I am out of order. I can be speaking in tongues over everybody without using earthly language. This is not telling someone face to face. If it is of the devil then cast it out, but if it is not, you better not. People are doing it and have done it all the time: kicking God out of the sanctuary!

"And even things without life giving sound, whether pipe or harp, except they give a distinction in the sounds, how shall it be known what is piped or harped? For if the trumpet give an uncertain sound, who shall prepare himself to the battle? So likewise ye, except ye utter by the tongue words easy to be understood, how shall it be known what is spoken? for ye shall speak into the air. There are, it may be, so many kinds of voices in the world, and none of them is without signification. Therefore if I know not the meaning of the voice, I shall be unto him that speaketh a barbarian, and he that speaketh shall be a barbarian unto me. Even so ye, forasmuch as ye are zealous of spiritual gifts, seek that ye may excel to the edifying of the church. Wherefore let him that speaketh in an unknown tongue pray that he may interpret."

So we first speak in tongues so we can be able to interpret it.

"For if I pray in an unknown tongue, my spirit prayeth, but my understanding is unfruitful. What is it then? I will pray with the spirit, and I will pray with the understanding also: I will sing with the spirit, and I will sing with the understanding also. Else when thou shalt bless with the spirit, how shall he that occupieth the room of the unlearned say Amen at thy giving of thanks, seeing he understandeth not what thou sayest? For thou verily givest thanks well, but the other is not edified. I thank my God, I speak with tongues more than ye all: Yet in the church I had rather speak five words with my understanding, that by my voice I might teach others also, than ten thousand words in an unknown tongue. Brethren, be not children in understanding: howbeit in malice be ye children, but in understanding be men."

You need to start praying in tongues, and then understanding will kick in. You can't stop praying in tongues just because your carnal mind cannot interpret it. A church without the gift is a church that is dead because the gift is the Holy Spirit. Paul thanks God for speaking in tongues more than all of them! He knew the importance of speaking it and also of understanding it because he was not just concerned about edifying himself but edifying the Body of Christ. Now you are saying that just because Paul has died, the Holy Spirit is not alive anymore? You better just rip out all the pages of the Bible that I am mentioning because if you don't believe in what the pages are saying, that is exactly what you are doing. Jesus is the living Word. You want to crucify Him again, but He cannot die ever again!

"In the law it is written, With men of other tongues and other lips will I speak unto this people; and yet for all that will they not hear me, saith the Lord. Wherefore tongues are for a sign, not to them that believe, but to them that believe not: but prophesying serveth not for them that believe not, but for them which believe. If therefore the whole church be come together into one place, and all speak with tongues, and there come in those that are unlearned, or unbelievers, will they not say that ye are mad?"

Be aware of those who don't believe, but don't stop speaking in tongues so they will hear it, they will believe it, and they will want it! The devil is a liar, not God.

"But if all prophesy, and there come in one that believeth not, or one unlearned, he is convinced of all, he is judged of all: And thus are the secrets of his heart made manifest; and so falling down on his face he will worship God, and report that God is in you of a truth. How is it then, brethren? when ye come together, every one of you hath a psalm, hath a doctrine, hath a tongue, hath a revelation, hath an interpretation. Let all things be done unto edifying."

Paul did not say stop. You are saying it is the devil, but God is saying it is Him! Every one of you has a psalm, a doctrine, and a TONGUE! Paul was making a plea not to be selfish so that when we come together we must build others up and build up the corporate church.

"If any man speak in an unknown tongue, let it be by two, or at the most by three, and that by course; and let one interpret."

Paul said to "keep speaking in tongues in the church, just do it in order." It came on me on that day and I keep doing it as Paul told us. Tongues are alive! It is not going to die! All we do is by the SAME SPIRIT! Healing, and all the other gifts, and tongues: done by the SAME SPIRIT! He is holy.

"But if there be no interpreter, let him keep silence in the church; and let him speak to himself, and to God."

There is a big IF, but you need to speak! If there is an interpreter!

"Let the prophets speak two or three, and let the other judge. If any thing be revealed to another that sitteth by, let the first hold his peace."

We are speaking about unknown tongues. Let's seal it as we read verses 36-40:

"What? came the word of God out from you? or came it unto you only? If any man think himself to be a prophet, or spiritual, let him acknowledge that the things that I write unto you are the commandments of the Lord. But if any man be ignorant, let him be ignorant. Wherefore, brethren, covet to prophesy, and forbid not to speak with tongues. Let all things be done decently and in order."

So you see above here another truth. Let's just repeat it. Will they see it? It does take the Holy Spirit. Pride and the Holy Spirit have no agreement and therefore have no communion. They said above: Don't stop speaking in tongues in their church. Just do it in order!

"For he that speaketh in an unknown tongue speaketh not unto men, but unto God: for no man understandeth him; howbeit in the spirit he speaketh mysteries."

Does God speak Greek, maybe Chinese, is it English? He speaks all things and understands all languages. That's why we call Him God. In Him, all things were made. So when we pray in tongues, we are also speaking the mysteries of heaven back to

God and commanding the heavenlies: the will of God! This is more scripture proof of the revelation of what Paul said in the book of Acts and what I mentioned at the beginning of this letter to the Church: they HEARD in their language. It did not say that they spoke in their language.

So people stay unlearned so they can't deny that tongues is written in the Word, but they lack wisdom and understanding; in that, they shut down and quench the Holy Spirit. The Bible says, "Do not quench the Spirit." Who made you the author of the Bible?

Jude speaks of them and also said we can pray in the Spirit! He actually said, "Holy Ghost," because He is a person on Earth, but you can't see Him but He is with us, as the Godhead.

"But, beloved, remember ye the words which were spoken before of the apostles of our Lord Jesus Christ; How that they told you there should be mockers in the last time, who should walk after their own ungodly lusts. These be they who separate themselves, sensual, having not the Spirit. But ye, beloved, building up yourselves on your most holy faith, praying in the Holy Ghost." Jude 17-20

They separate themselves from those with the Spirit when they say that there is no gift anymore and that it is of the past. You will not shut down our own encounter with the Holy Spirit. It is way better when you preach the Gospel with the tongue of the Spirit. Pray in the Holy Spirit!!! Build yourself up! Interpret it, and you will edify that person!

So when we pray in the Holy Spirit, it will also build us up. We may not fully understand what we are praying in the Spirit, but the Spirit knows it. In **Romans**, God talks about just groanings and sounds.

"Likewise the Spirit also helpeth our infirmities: for we know not what we should pray for as we ought: but the Spirit itself maketh intercession for us with groanings which cannot be uttered. And he that searcheth the hearts knoweth what is the mind of the Spirit, because he maketh intercession for the saints according to the will of God." Romans 8:26-27

The Spirit makes noises that the carnal mind can't understand it. He is making intercession for us. Pray in tongues. Sometimes when you keep praying in your earthly language, you pray to the wind sometimes, but when you pray in the Spirit, there is no time wasted. Only the Spirit intercedes for us the will of God! How perfect is that?

So interceding is doing it for you. This word is Word. But those who have gotten the gift of tongues know what it was for. God gave it to them knowing that others would mock, hate, and call it from the devil. Are you calling the Holy Spirit the devil? It is a serious thing to speak as one who knows all and call one's treasure demonic. The Pharisees and Sadducees did the same thing. They called holy as unholy!

We have both the Word of God and the encounter. All of us can remember the day we got it because it came with fire! It is amazing! When I was a baby Christian who out of the purity of my heart was asking for the Holy Spirit as in **Matthew chapter 7**, and He gave me the gift, you are saying God is a liar and He gave me a serpent (devil). I think God is clarifying who is really deceived.

Since the Holy Spirit came on me with speaking in tongues, I cast demons out all over the world. Jesus said Satan can't cast out Satan. Since the evidence of speaking in tongues, I have been free from all of the lust of the flesh, and all the things I used to do, I no longer do. Jesus said you will know my disciples by their fruit, not by what scriptures they think they know. I will live by these signs and wonders proceeding from the TRUTH, the Word. We speak with new tongues. Do you? Not everyone who says they are a believer really believes because you cannot believe in Jesus and deny His power and His gifts. It's a total package deal.

Search your heart and humble yourself under His mighty hand. We must love God and not come against His Word. Pride is dividing the Body as they exalt heresies above the Word of God. We are one Spirit, one doctrine, one baptism, and in Him there is no division. Keep the unity of the faith, in love!

{

When Satan gets in your heart (offense, rebellion, hate, jealousy), he will turn your holy kisses into kisses of betrayal and entrapment and make you give up on love for his cause and will destroy your destiny. Satan will make you feel right because you have exalted your negative agreement above the Word of God (love), making you God. This is why we need one another. If we begin to hate each other and devour one another, we are no longer messengers of the cross but anti-Christ.

....

Too many so-called Christians hear the Truth and continue in their personal agendas above the Truth. Seems to me many Christians don't have the Spirit of Truth. If they do, then their WILL rules them and not the Spirit of Truth. This eliminates any possibility to become a son of God. God does not force Himself on any man. That's the beauty of the cross. It doesn't discriminate. It doesn't judge. It's there for whoever chooses to pick it up. God will not pick it up for you. He already did. It is finished.

"They began to relate their experiences on the road and how He was recognized by them in the breaking of the bread."

Luke 24:35

THE THREE TOWERS
Rebellion - Pride - Witchcraft

In this writing, I am going to focus on the attitude of the heart. You will see how our actions create unhealthy situations and how bad decisions can create a long life of trouble or can even take us to where God has never intended us to go. To do so, I will be using a specific character in the Bible: Cain.

God rejected Cain because of his heart. When we get angry at God, we turn on one another and start hating our brother and sister. Cain was not obeying God. He did what he was supposed to do from the outside, but from the inside the heart was wrong. If the heart is wrong, we won't receive the blessing of doing it. God said to Cain, "If you do well, you will be received. But if you don't, sin lies at the door."

Our attitude shows our gratitude. Jealousy consumed Cain and made him a murderer. It brought him to a dry land. He was feeling miserable. Our actions always bring consequences. When we get in the flesh, we get the consequences of the flesh: death. The Spirit is life.

Abel was not doing anything wrong. It was actually Cain that had the problem, and he was taking it out on Abel. When God is trying to correct us, we can become rebellious or we can become fruitful.

We are supposed to be our brother's keeper. The spirit of murder, religion, all started from Cain because he had a religious attitude with his offering. Now, we are the offering to God. We bring our hearts. Our daily sacrifice: you and your cross!

Satan is the father of pride. Everyone with pride always wants to be the one who is right. In pride, we don't even hear the other, but we are already resisting Truth. Now, we need to break the mold of Cain. We need to break the mold of the old man. The blood of Abel cries out but how much louder is the blood of Jesus?

Pride only listens to its own heart and puts up walls because it does not want to be exposed. That jealousy killed Abel. This is what we see with one another. These three things: rebellion, pride, and witchcraft go hand and hand. Pride births rebellion and rebellion brings an atmosphere of witchcraft.

Abraham heard from God Himself but did not wait on God. He followed the suggestion of his wife. The world was turned upside down because of this one mistake: Ishmael. Don't think that because you are His that you can't create your own Ishmael. Abraham lacked judgment. His faith failed him at that time because he followed his flesh. He got in negative agreement with His wife even to the point of fornication just to make a promise come to pass. What started in the spirit ended in the flesh. He had to wait 13 years, the number of rebellion, to see promise. Don't let our flesh get us off course. Don't let pride say, "It can't happen to me."

Ishmael will create problems in the church and in your own life. Ishmael is a fruit of rebellion and pride. Disobedience is as the sin of witchcraft. Don't think your mistakes won't have consequences. If Abraham wanted to do it his own way and to help God, that is a sign of pride and brought heavy consequences!

The problem with rebellion is that we want it when we want it, and we don't want to wait on God to give us what He wants and when He wants it. Or not obeying God when He tells us to do something. Hesitation is also disobedience. We need to get this thing out! Rebellion is the breeding ground for many Ishmaels. We need to break the mold and follow Christ and not Cain.

The power of agreement is manifested when two come together. Abraham and Sarah experienced it but in a wrong way: negative agreement. Two with negative agreement will put ten thousand to flight as well! Negative agreement is a work of the flesh. Positive agreement is a work of the Spirit.

Sometimes we are looking at the messenger and we are forgetting who is speaking through that one, and pride will not listen to anybody until they listen to God for themselves. God told Saul what to do and Saul did some of what God said. He also did what Samuel was supposed to do, the sacrifice. In the end, Samuel had to do what Saul did not do.

God said to Saul: Kill all! But Saul kept Agag, the king. He took that seed of the enemy and kept it. It is the same thing: God is saying, "Kill all," but you want to do it your way and keep what He is telling you to kill. Sometimes we go where God sends us, but then we do it our way.

It grieved Samuel, and it grieves us, too, because we know there will be consequences for people's pride. We see it, but they ignore it. God points out the way through His Word, but they don't follow it. Samuel interceded for Saul all night because he even kept some sheep. Saul began to lie and believed that he was right. Rebellion takes people's discernment and destroys it. Saul believed that he obeyed, but he had put himself under witchcraft because he did not do exactly what God told him to do. Pride came in in Saul's life.

Sometimes, we do just a little bit of what God tells us. When we are being tested, the master (teacher) stays quiet. It is easier to follow God when we are dead. When we are crucified, it is easier to obey God. There is no resistance. God can turn it all around if we take one trip to the cross. God said to Saul that there was a season that he was little in his own eyes. God wanted him to know that pride had consumed him and made him his own god. Then God repented that He had ever made Saul king.

If grace is lifting that means that pride is rising and that rebellion is rising. God gives grace only to the humble. This is a great thermometer for pride. When relationships get hard, when you start striving, check yourself. Pride cuts grace right out of the way.

Obedience is better than sacrifice. You may be doing this and that, but you are doing it out of works, not out of obedience. Your heart is not in it. Because of that, you will never be able to win God's heart. Look at Cain.

"I don't need an apostle. I don't need a prophet," Saul thought. "I'm king. I'm anointed." He tried to do his own thing through his own anointing, but God is very much concerned about order. When we break the order, we break God's heart. When someone is rebelling, witchcraft follows you wherever you go. You put it on people – you don't mean it – but it is just a natural effect. You say, "What changed here at the church, in my family, or in my job? Things are not the same," but it is coming from you because you are exalting your ways above His. Obedience is always better than anything else you do. If you are not doing exactly what He told you, He won't receive even the things that you are sacrificing for Him.

Stubbornness is stiff-neckedness. It is as the sin of iniquity. Don't you think that God will not reject your anointing? Everybody is beating themselves up because they are not doing what they are told to do. Most of our problem is that we decide to exalt our hearts above His. "I did this, I did that," but it does not matter. God can use a mule to fulfill his purpose. You may be still under rebellion doing things on the outside, but most of the rebellion is coming from the inside of your heart. Rebellion is anti-Christ and an enemy of the cross, and it suffocates love.

All of us have anointing and authority but that can be contaminated through rebellion. "I have to look good," but there is no repentance. You did not change your mind. You just want to look good in front of people. Pride wants you looking good with fig leaves, but we need to be worried about how God looks at us when we are in rebellion. Saul's pride was so strong when he was corrected by Samuel. All he cared was about was what he looked like to the people.

Samuel ended up doing what Saul was supposed to do. Samuel had to do what Saul should have done from the beginning. Secretly repentance won't work. Sometimes God will use a prophet to kill what you are not capable of because you are blind and under your own witchcraft. Saul had so much pride. He was incapable of repenting.

When you get stiff-necked, you are really rebelling against God, one another, and His Word. Miriam had leprosy because she rebelled against the Man of God. We get too comfortable when God speaks through someone else. God is for us, but if we are against Him, who will be for us?

Did the Holy Spirit come out of Stephen like a ghost? No. He was a natural man full of His Spirit. They were killing God in Him. They were rebelling, rejecting, and resisting the Holy Spirit. The Word compares them to Jannes and Jambres, the magicians of Egypt (**2 Timothy 3:8**). They are always resisting, even those who are telling the Truth. They are always resisting God's Word and His direction. That level of rebellion got all the prophets before Stephen killed. Only those who are able to obey and follow Him are the humble.

Threefold cord: pride, rebellion, and witchcraft. They work together. I have never seen one without the others. When people are rebelling, and you bring the Truth, they gnash their teeth. The power of negative agreement can make you a murderer. You begin even to hate people that are close to your heart. Just like when Stephen spoke. They killed Stephen because of truth. He called them all rebellious, saying that they always resist the truth.

Stephen remembered what Jesus said and did the same: "Forgive them. They don't know what they are doing." What Jesus said, Stephen said, "Lay not their sin on their account." Stephen thought, "I cannot be offended right now. I will do anything so my heart can stay pure." And in holiness, he released his spirit, just like Jesus did, and saw the glory of God.

Now Judas was looking for negative agreement in the enemy camp. He did not agree with what and how Jesus wanted to do God's business. If Satan can get in a heart of someone to be against a perfect leader like Jesus, how much more do you think Satan could get in our hearts because of our imperfect brothers and leaders? How much more do we need to be careful? Judas had that entrapment spirit. We don't go to the cross. We keep the list of wrongdoing ready when we are being confronted, and we start pulling things out of the treasure chest. We say love covers, but, actually, love eliminates even the record of sin done to and through us!

Loves does not just cover sin. Love dissolves it. Also, loves does not keep a record of wrong. You keep hiding that list of wrongdoing for later use. "He said, she said..." We don't have time for that. Your laundry list needs to be burned.

Satan first put things into Judas' heart: division, jealousy, strife, etc. And later on, he took over his whole being. When you have something against someone, sometimes nobody knows but that person does. Judas, for the last time, heard the message during the last supper and did not repent, and Satan entered into his heart! God gave him warnings. But the funny thing is that the humble ones were asking, "Is it me?"

When Jesus was washing his disciples' feet, Peter first said, "I am not worthy of you washing my feet." Then Jesus corrected him, and he received the correction and said, "Wash not only my feet but my hands and head and my whole body." That is the attitude He wants from us.

When you are rebelling, you stop seeing the little hints of correction that He is giving you throughout the way. We cannot walk in love and in rebellion at the same time.

In rebellion, you break communion with God. You can't hear Him. You may be hearing Jezebel, but not Him. The only cure for rebellion is the fear of the Lord. Judas played the game all the way to the end. He was being nice to Jesus, but from the outside, he had his heart contaminated. Judas' rebellion took his life, exactly the same way Saul's rebellion took his life: suicide. That is what Satan wants us to commit: spiritual suicide – killing our destinies.

Satan wants our heart. God wants our heart. We need to guard it at all times, or Satan will begin to try to poison our hearts. If you want to win against these three towers – rebellion, pride, and witchcraft – you need to fight as a warrior. Guard that heart with every bit of your strength. In doing so, the three towers will become like crumbs if you humble yourself under His mighty hand!

BREAKING BREAD

Genesis 4:1-4, Genesis 16, 1 Samuel 15, Nehemiah 9, Mark 14:1-12, John 13, 2 Timothy 3, Hebrews 10:20-39

EDOM CAMP

Edom means "red" in the Hebrew language, derived from Esau, Isaac's eldest son, who sold his birthright for red pottage. His descendants were the Edomites who were great enemies of Israel (**Psalm 83:5**).

It is impossible to hang in the enemy's camp and not to begin to think like the enemy. Do you realize this is why Jesus said to hate the world? Why is it the enemy's camp? His camp is negative, and when we begin to connect and to stay there, our agreements with it become negative. We are in the world but not of the world but in Christ. This is why Jesus said let the dead bury the dead. The world operates from the tree of the knowledge of good and evil. They will justify their actions by their own understanding. They will bring in their own righteousness void of the cross.

This is why we have carnal (worldly) churches. Jesus said I have called you out of the world. Any church or Christian organization that does not preach the cross will be deceived. So many get mad at the TRUTH and, in that, Satan starts to pervert the Gospel with their own understanding, slowly deceiving themselves. As pride slips in, TRUTH slips out.

When we begin to be an enemy of the cross, we begin to be enemies with those who preach the cross, adhere to the cross, and live by the cross. The world says, "Me, me, me." The cross says, "Him, Him, Him." Satan's strategy is to get you to deny the cross and pick his way. When we get offended at the Word, we get offended at Jesus Himself. That is who He is. Where we are led by our feelings, our feelings will bring us into the wilderness, into a dry land. Do not give up on love because love never gave up on you. Do not underestimate the devil because that is pride, too. Grace is right where you left it, right at the cross. Without the cross, you will live and not die, but to die is to gain and without the cross, there is no glory. Today, remember to pick up your cross and follow love, and grace is right there.

"This is the bread which cometh down from heaven, that a man may eat thereof, and not die."

....

John 6:50-71

SPIRIT OF ENTRAPMENT

Word from God preceding a dream:

"Dream: I was next to my car and this person next to me that I know was representing an entrapping spirit. They would throw a crack rock in my car and then I would frantically look for it and get out because you know that in the world it says that possession is 9/10 of the law. (God speaks to me through my life experiences that what we all have is our own dream languages. His dreams are always personal or revelation or warning or correction. It's His voice. You cannot use formulas or grids.) So this is what the person was doing, back and forth and back and forth. Then getting very frustrated, I began to get tired. I called 911. Then as I was throwing it out of the car, I looked down, and there next to my car, I saw that someone had a pile of my paperwork, some things with my ID on it. Wow, now crack in a pile with all this stuff with my name on it. I was like, 'Will the police believe me with my reputation of doing the right thing and of all my work for God and the Kingdom?' Then the police came. It was a set-up. The person was working with the corrupt authority, and it was a family member of the person." Then I knew that we can even fight against flesh and blood if someone is bent on division, discord, and offense. They become agents of destruction.

Here is the word of God: Satan will work with familiar spirits to slander you and your name with the accuser of the brethren. This is how it works. Then God showed me a vision of the ministry of Jesus. This spirit will work with people in pride or offense that refuse to repent. They want to but don't know how because pride blinds all. It's what they look like that matters to them more than anything, and they see everyone else as wrong. There are no people as prideful as Pharisees and Sadducees. Leviathan gets a hold of a person because they are not humbling their ways and agendas to love and the cross. They become double agents and don't even realize it because the plot, the plan, and the execution were motivated not by love but by selfish desires of what they wanted, and they made a negative agreement. Satan got a hold of Judas this way and began to despise Jesus. But remember, Jesus had no fault. This entrapment spirit will find fault even in perfection. Look at our master.

Cars represent ministries usually, like in this case in my dream. God said that Satan is out to destroy ministries, families, and destinies. He can only do it when he can use someone to work with him. Satan wanted to kill Jesus so it's a spirit of murder, but he did not know he was playing right into God's hand and plan. Killing Jesus robbed himself of all the power and authority he was given. Whenever Judas was around the others, he would stir up indignation. He could not find solid negative agreement so he went to the enemy's camp. The religious rulers agreed to betray Jesus and set Him up. He will use married couples to make negative agreements that kill them. Look at Ananias and Sapphira. Peter confronted them: **"Then Peter said unto her, "How is it that ye have agreed together to tempt the Spirit of the Lord? Behold, the feet of them which have buried thy husband are at the door, and shall carry thee out" (Acts 5:9).** So he used the false authority of the accusers of Jesus. Jesus is the authority because He is the Word made flesh. This is the book of the law.

Judas hated correction and began to be offended at Jesus. So he went to leviathan's camp.

We can be entrapped because we love someone so much that we open ourselves up to help them, and we put ourselves in a vulnerable position because Satan will say whatever you say. I will use it against you in my court of accusation, and I will pervert it and twist it and make you look like a villain, and I will demonize you. Just like someone who wants something so bad, like a drug addict or a person full of lust, that they fall into the trap and get set up by the police in the world. In this spirit, the enemy will set you up. Have you ever said, "Man, all I was doing was trying to help them, and it all got turned around on me?" That is twisting entrapment. Somewhere, when you get solicited by the devil because you want that person to so be free or longsuffering as they will not repent, then the twister begins to twist what you said and what you meant and tries to make you look like the wrong, bad one. You want the cross and for the person so much to see and to be restored that you can be trapped in leviathan's court with them when you get in their net with them. But God is the final authority. He knows that everything in darkness will be manifested by the light. So keep on loving, preaching, and teaching, but be very careful.

"In meekness instructing those that oppose themselves; if God peradventure will give them repentance to the acknowledging of the truth; And that they may recover themselves out of the snare of the devil, who are taken captive by him at his will." 2 Timothy 2:25-26

These brood of vipers have been working with Satan to entrap Jesus ever since He read Isaiah and said this word is fulfilled this day. He shut the book and walked out, and they wanted to kill Him from that day on. If you are in covenant with Jesus, if you have an anointing, and if you are a truth bearer, I have news for you. He wants to kill you, too. He will use the most familiar people around you. They won't even realize they are being ensnared. When Satan puts an idea, a seed, or a plan in your heart, and you bring it to another person, it's on. Negative agreement will blind all parties. They believe they are doing the right thing. It's called deception, and offense is the bait of Satan, and he works with children of disobedience. Satan did not like Judas. He just used him, and then killed him. So, false accusations, false discernment, and hidden motives are all the work of darkness. That's what was in Judas' heart. To others, they thought he must have gone off to get supplies for the poor, but he was heading to entrap Jesus with the law, but it was not the law of love. Judas even wanted to look good in front of the others. He kissed Jesus like he was for Him, but his plan was betrayal. They give nice words on your wall, little sweet gestures, but their heart has a hidden plan.

That is what offense unrepented will do – make you betray all and believe you are right in your cause going to false authority to help build your case against a brother or sister or to make yourself look like the victim. But all those who spiritually discern and know exactly what Satan is up to will expose him. If we exalt our feelings and our desires above God's government and God's truth, we become a puppet to the master of lies and deception, killing love in our life, and crucifying the Jesus in our brothers and sisters. Love does not take record of wrong. Love does not ignore someone. Love does not cut communication with those around them. Love does not exalt anything above the Spirit of Truth. Love never fails, never gives up, or quits, endures all things and obeys God right to the cross. When we put love for the sake of self and move from God's Word, then pride comes before the snares of the devil. Next thing you know, you are dining with Jezebel and building cases against others for your own plans and secrets and end up falling in God's hands.

"It is a fearful thing to fall into the hands of the living God." Hebrews 10:31

Leviathan will twist intentions and motives and use its victims to entrap God's beloved. The cross will crush his head. See, Judas didn't even realize he was wrong because he wanted something so bad that it corrupted his thinking. This word was a warning of how severe disobedience and not submitting oneself to the cross are and what Satan will do. He comes to steal, kill, and destroy you and hand you over to him if what you want becomes stronger and greater than what God wants. God just gave me His definition of Leviathan: It is the power of division, ultimately divisive and anti-unity. Let's put off every sin that so easily entangles us and fear the Lord, love and be loved in Jesus' name. I pray to break discord, disloyalty, division, dysfunction, disillusions, divorce, dishonesty, and distrust all in the name of Jesus! Amen!!

"That every one of you should know how to possess his vessel in sanctification and honour; Not in the lust of concupiscence, even as the Gentiles which know not God: That no man go beyond and defraud his brother in any matter: because that the Lord is the avenger of all such, as we also have forewarned you and testified. For God hath not called us unto uncleanness, but unto holiness. He therefore that despiseth, despiseth not man, but God, who hath also given unto us his holy Spirit. But as touching brotherly love ye need not that I write unto you: for ye yourselves are taught of God to love one another." 1 Thessalonians 4:4-9

{

Realize there are a lot of people saying the right things but for the wrong reasons. If what you are saying is for or out of a wrong heart, even if it is right, it is wrong. God is getting me to not only discern truth and lies but also to discern the motive. This is very important because things can carry witchcraft. If what you do is not all for Him and love and repair, you will begin to operate in a wrong spirit. Not everyone is saying everything right. What we are doing is what really matters and who and what we are doing it for. There is only one agenda in the Kingdom of God and that is HIS, and it cannot be you, me, or anyone but Him! We must discern what is behind even truth.

"And when one of them that sat at meat with him heard these things, he said unto him, Blessed [is] he that shall eat bread in the kingdom of God."

Luke 14:15

WILL YOU BE MY NEIGHBOR?

Who is your neighbor? Anyone in your vicinity. Jesus said: "Love your neighbor as yourself." But if you don't have God's love, your love is like worldly love. If you do love, you live. Love equals living. If you don't love, you will die. There is no division in love. God said to love Him and to obey Him. When we do that, the love of God is in us. Love is the cross.

Love does not move by emotion. Love is not an emotion. Love is self-control. Love has compassion on those moving on emotion, but love does not rely on emotion. We have the Holy Spirit, the healing balm. We are totally capable of loving our neighbor. It is the Holy Spirit that allows us to love unconditionally and without selfish desires. When we walk in the Spirit, we walk in love.

God says we need to learn to love people even outside the family of Christ that He has given us. Sometimes even among ourselves, we have problems with loving. Sometimes we see our brother hurting, but we don't stop to love on them. Even the Good Samaritan was more loving than His own people during Jesus' time. The Levite and the priest just ignored their neighbor in need.

Obedience shows that you love God, not smiles, not flattering, not emotions. Everybody loves themselves, but they don't love their neighbor as themselves. Then we see it is all about us. If you love yourself more than God, you are not seeing that it is all about them. Loving God first allows us to love others.

Religious people hang around a belief, but the remnant are always hanging on the cross. Love is not just being nice. Love is not just saying, "That a boy! Keep going. You are going to make it!" Love is not a pat on the back. Love looks like something. Love looks like the cross. Love denies self. This is why we preach the cross because without the cross we will never love like Christ or look like Christ.

False love is selfish. Real love is denying yourself for the sake of others.

The Bible says, "Owe no man nothing but to love them." How can you submit to the earthly ordinances and not submit yourself to His Word? Put on His cross, and you will be able to love. We will always give provision for the flesh if we don't. I don't want to hang around believers but around disciples of Jesus because these are the ones fulfilling the law of God at all times. Only when we pick up our cross are we able to be what He has died for us to be.

When you start to do what you are supposed to do, you become their enemy. You are picking up your cross but the others are not. Then here comes division. How can you love God and not pick up your cross? This is why Jesus preached about it. He came to bring division between real love (God love) and false love (the love of the World).

Ignorance is bliss? But once you read the Word, you are not ignorant anymore. You know exactly what to do. But if you decide to do what is right, even when they are trying to find fault in you, that won't be able to touch you. The Word says that love covers a multitude of sins. Love does not pay back evil for evil. It is impossible. If we start losing our peace and being tossed to and fro, it is because we are not picking up our cross for the sake of love. We can't hold on to it. It is impossible to be picking up your cross at the same time you are picking up offense.

God will always defend love. Love denies. It denies lies. It denies the right to be right. It denies the flaws in others. It denies the flesh. It denies self-will. It denies gathering evidence on someone else to prove its case.

Feeding the poor on the street is not love. It is kindness. It is mercy. Real love is the turning of the cheek. There are a lot of works of justice that are out of love. You can do mission trips every month and have no profit in your life according to **1 Corinthians 13**.

Love does not get jealous of somebody that is getting the benefits of the cross when you are not willing to pick up your own. We get provoked so easily. That is not love. If you love, offense does not stick. People were trying to catch Jesus all the time. They got angry at Him because He never got out of the road of love. Love rejoices in the Truth. If you resist Truth, you don't have love. If you welcome Truth, love is in you. Love is Truth. Jesus said: "Do you love me?" How will I know? "When you obey My Word and lay down your will and life."

Anything that talks about Jesus does not mean that it is the Gospel. The Gospel without the cross and without repentance is not the Gospel. It is only a belief system.

Many people gather around a belief that they agree on, but there is no power when we avoid the cross. The cross is authentic. When you repent is it not because you know you need to? It is a matter of going to the cross and doing what you were not doing or obeying. Then the power of the cross and the blood allow you and empower you to obey.

You always win in love. God always defends love. It may look like you failed, but if you abide in love, it does not matter the outcome: You are a winner. We have to love through it all! Love your enemies. Bless them that curse you. This will win all the time. You feel like you are losing, but believe me, you are winning.

Love dies for its brother. Jesus did that for us. The firstborn among many brethren! Just obey the Word. There is no way to pick up our cross in our own strength. Love does not put itself above others.

Everybody wants the honor that comes from God, but that only comes from the cross. It is not easy but it is worth it. You want favor? Go to the cross. You want blessings? Pick up your cross. You want to defeat Satan? Pick up your cross.

Who are your mother, your brother, and father? Those who do the will of God. If they are of us, they must be with us. If they are not with us, they must be not of us. You can see a natural division happening in the body or church. It is between carnality and the Spirit.

I want to live the 70 x 70 love. Oh, your brother hurt you? How many times should you love them? 70 x 70. How many times should you forgive your brother? 70 x 70. How many times should you give another chance? 70 x 70. People who make excuses for not forgiving are denying the cross. People giving up on people are giving up on the cross.

Jesus did it all for us He never gave up on us, but now we need to get the benefit of the cross as we do what He did. Take up your cross, daily. Daily! Lose your life for the sake of your neighbor. If you do this, pick up your cross, you will always see the manifestation of His resurrection. Keep putting on Christ. Give no provision for your flesh which is anti-Christ and anti-your brother! This is the spirit of Cain when you think you love God but are actually hating your brother.

Your own righteousness will cause you to think that you are something or are right, but you are still nothing. You are still denying the cross. You don't want to die for the sake of others. Take communion with the cross. Eat His flesh. Drink His blood. Day by day.

Without the cross, what do you get? A reprobate mind. The power of the cross means nothing to others, but to us who believe it is the power unto salvation. We need to surrender everything. You can get an "amen" when you mention the blessings but not when you mention the cross! Woe unto me if I don't preach the cross. Woe unto me if I preach only belief and leave all the other parts of the Gospel out. The cross makes us partners with His sufferings.

The fellowship of His suffering will make us uncomfortable still to the resurrection of the dead, but we have to pick up the cross. We need to weep when we see our brothers not picking up their cross. They became enemies of the cross. If you don't pick up your cross, you can't have His because they are one.

His commandment is that we love one another and lay down our lives for them. Show your life not by what you give but by what you give up. "Not my will but your will be done"...This is

His will for us: Love! But there is no true love without you hanging yourself on the cross! When you have your cross, you fulfill **1 Corinthians 13** to its fullness.

Persecution identifies that you are with Him. Keep on loving. Keep on picking up the cross. If we do righteously, we are righteous. Do the right thing by taking up your cross. You will see the benefits of it here on earth. There is no depression in death because you are dead. There is no anxiety in death because you are dead. There is no worry in death because you are dead. If people break covenant with you, they are breaking covenant with the cross. They are taking back their life. Jesus said, "Lose this life and gain His life." The cross is where you lose to win.

Don't leave your cross at home. Go back and pick it up! Pride does not stay on the cross. Whoever does not love your brother is a murderer. We ought to lay down our lives for our brother. If we are laying down our lives for one another, every day, there is no offense, there is no division, and there is no strife. There is no argument because there is no flesh ruling you on the cross.

The Gospel is really good news, but not good news for your flesh. You have to crucify it. We are not to love in word but in deed and in the Truth.

If our hearts condemn us, God is greater than our hearts. Keep His commandments: Love your brother! Pick up your cross! Do these two things that please God: Believe on His name and love one another! Because He gave us these commandments!

Anti-Christ is anti-Word. When we don't want to obey His Word, we are anti-Word. If we don't love our brother, we are anti-our brother! The cross perfects love. On a good day or on a bad day, how much do you love your brother? When they deserve it or not, how do you love them? That is what He is asking you. Do you love me? Take up your cross. Do you love me? Deny yourself.

Let us love one another because love is of God, and everyone that loves is born of God! If you love not, you know not God. Deny yourself: That is love! When you are feeling left out, you deny yourself for the sake of them! If God so loved us, we ought to love one another! If we love one another, God dwells in us! And because of that, the love of God is being seen in Spirit and in Truth.

When you pick up your cross, God dwells in you. When you lay down your life, God dwells in you. When you deny yourself, God dwells in you. That kind of love is the true love of God dwelling in us all. He that dwells in love dwells in Him and Him in them. Let us love each other just as Christ loves the Church. He that loves their brother loves God as well.

There is no glory without the cross. Do you realize that Jesus was telling everyone to pick up their cross even before He even did it Himself, but He was doing it in His heart constantly even until the full manifestation? He was already doing it as He was still living. He was saying if you want to follow me to where I am going, you need to do what I am doing. He was prophesying over Himself constantly. This is why and how we know the Word of God is so powerful. We preach the cross so we will pick it up.

This is why Jesus said, "There is no greater love than this: to lay down your life for your brother." So this is real love: the cross. And the cross fulfills all the law. Anything we do around the cross is just belief. But being a partaker of the cross is being a partaker of His divine nature. This is living in freedom. This is the fullness of life. This is peace, and this is the communion with God and man, not religion. This communion is one union between us and Him. It is true covenant.

So let us not just love in word (lip service) or in thought, but love in Truth. This is the only Gospel unto salvation: that we obey Him. To obey Him is to love Him, and to love Him is to partake with Him by giving Him our lives for His divine exchange. The Good News is this: Grace empowers us to become the sons of God. Every seed must fall to the ground and die to reproduce life. Will you be one of His lambs led to the slaughter? Or will you fight for your old man until you die and end up never living in the glory that He died for us to have? Will you be my neighbor?

BREAKING BREAD

Luke 10:25-37, Mark 12:28-34, Romans 13, 1 Peter 4:1-10, 1 Corinthians 13, John 12: 24, Luke 9:22-25, Matthew 16:24-26, Philippians 3:7-14, John 15:8-20, 1 John 3, 1 John 4

BETRAYAL

We must know that betrayal is unavoidable, but what is avoidable is you being a betrayer. Why God hates betrayal is that it is the most destructive and hurtful thing. It is straight at the heart. The scriptures are full of it. Jesus never betrayed anyone at any time. Neither should we. Loyalty is one of the biggest things in the Old and New Testament that God honors! David was even loyal to Saul even when He was not. Jesus was loyal to His disciples all the way to the cross, even when some of them were not. God says He sets a table in front of our enemies.

The thing with Jesus was that He walked with Judas over three years. He ate with him, spent numerous hours with Him, and loved Him literally to death. That's what betrayal looks like: when everyone is around you and everything seems well, but the person you trusted, who you poured into, who you opened yourself up to in some intimate ways sharing secrets of the heart, you find out that they are using your openness against you. Betrayal is broken trust and deceit. In Peter's case, it was denying Jesus. That was not as big a deal because when you deny someone, it's usually out of fear. That is about not showing up for a fight or sticking up for your buddy when people are attacking. Betrayal is hidden deception, walking as if nothing is wrong when the whole time, you are plotting your exit and no else knows your sneakiness, but God knows even our thoughts.

This is what betrayal does: It doesn't stab you in the back. It stabs you right in the heart as it smiles at you and tells you how wonderful and amazing you are. It comes out of nowhere. If you are not heavy on discernment, it will wreck you and blindside you. The betrayer does not just hurt the one it betrays but the entire tribe, family, church, or workplace. When you are betrayed, it will put witchcraft out to the carnal because they think everything looks right on the outside and brings confusion to people, even making the victim look like the guilty one, making others around them think and wonder what they must have done to them to make them leave or walk out of marriages and covenant relationships while the whole time demonizing the real victim. This is what betrayal does. It's anti-LOVE.

Satan likes to bring confusion. Confusion opens up for gossip and secondary offense or third party offenses. So the betrayer makes a mess that affects the entire family, breaking commitments. Husband betrays wife and everyone suffers from the kids all the way down to the dog or vice versa, a wife that cheats and runs off as well. This is why God hates it. That is why God said, "I hate divorce," because it hurts everyone. You don't need to be married to have a DIVIDE or divorce. You just need to be committed, that is to be in covenant relationship with another such as the body of Christ or marriages or work commitments. God loves faithfulness in every area of our lives. It is a great character thermometer. Jesus says every hidden thing will come to the light. When Jesus said to Judas, "You betray with a kiss," what He was saying was, "Wow, you want to look good to the family that is breaking up." That brought much confusion. Kisses are an act of affection. So more than ever, Jesus says you honor with your lips but your heart is against me. This came down from literal lips. Jesus was like, "You're turning me in to be killed, trying to look like a good guy to everyone around you. That is so, so selfish, Judas. For what? For thirty pieces of silver? Really?" Money was not the real reason. It was the icing on the cake. It was his rebellion to Jesus and word that brought him to be infiltrated by the devil. Really, that's all I was worth to you? All the nights I stayed up with you praying? Fasting, praying for your family, and trips to your loved ones because they were in need? All the long walks where I told you all about me? I gave you all my authority and power in my name. Then it's an empty seat that never gets filled at the table, the dinner table, the conference table. With Judas, it was the table of the Lord. The emptiness of betrayal has a place in the heart that no one else can fill because you gave it freely.

Betrayal, the nastiest thing even in the world! Jesus warns us that we will be betrayed. Don't be shocked. Just make sure you are not the one selling out. The first thing that happens when you are betrayed, fear comes in. You feel it in the pit of your stomach. Then all of a sudden, there's frustration, then despair, and then disappointment. Then you play things back in your mind over and over again wondering what was it? That's witchcraft.

The crazy thing is you're never prepared for betrayal. It's like a shock. Then the enemy will play with your mind and make you feel responsible, but you're still the victim because they are gone, and you are left picking up the pieces. Then you can't gossip so you need to move in love. This is longsuffering, not only putting yourself back together but everyone else who has been affected. It is anti-Love and denies the cross, not itself. People who betray people are full of themselves and overtaken by pride.

Father, I pray I never, ever betray anyone. Father, give us clean hands and a pure heart. Let us see you in everyone and every situation. Let us always be part of the solution, the deliverance, and the righteous way. Keep us from evil. Bless all those who persecute us.

**"Cast thy bread upon the waters:
for thou shalt find it after many days."**

....

Ecclesiastes 1:11

DREAMS AND VISIONS

God's voice comes in many different ways: the written Word, the still small voice within, dreams and visions, prophetic unctions, etc. People who don't have the fear of the Lord start despising them. God speaks through them but people are ignoring them. When you do that, you are quenching the Spirit within others. The Word said, "Do not quench the Holy Spirit," and "Don't be ignorant concerning spiritual gifts." When we quench the Spirit, we are shutting down direction, warning, and protection, and we become blind to the things in the dark that are being manifested by the light. God reveals the secrets and the hidden motives of people as well. It's like knowing before it comes to pass. It's amazing.

1 Thessalonians 5: 20 says, **"Despise not prophesying."** All these spiritual gifts are to profit all men. The gift of revelation operates through dreams and visions. The word of knowledge only comes from God, and God will have those who can interpret them when God reveals things to some and others may not see it. Not everybody that gets dreams is a prophet but every prophet (office) gets dreams. God may speak to you in the wilderness, one on one, but He will also speak to you through somebody else however He wants to.

When we only want to hear God by ourselves, we despise prophecy. A wise man will receive the instruction of wisdom through somebody else. The other name for the Holy Spirit is wisdom. A wise man will hear God however He speaks and will increase in learning and knowledge. Obtain counsel but wise counsel. If you know that there is a prophet among you and a body full of gifts, then that is the place where you are supposed to get counsel from. If you hear it and receive it, you receive the rewards and the benefits of it, and you will increase in learning. The fear of the Lord is the foundation of wisdom. If you don't fear the Lord, you will not fear the unction from the Holy One.

Paul said, "Do not despise revelatory gifts. Do not despise prophesying." Pride will say: "I will get counsel on my own." Wisdom cries out all around you, and you walk right by it. The sad thing, many will seek counsel from people they know will tell them what they want to hear when wisdom is sitting right next to you, but you despise it. This is one of the reasons why God told us not to forsake the assembling together because there is protection in the real Bride, not dead assemblies of religion but body ministry with gifts within all to profit all. He will pour out His Spirit upon you: the Spirit of the Lord and the spirits of wisdom, of understanding, of counsel, of might, of knowledge, and of the fear of the LORD. But rebellious people will be led by their own way. A lot of sheep have decided to hear Him one way. Some will look up and down in the Bible, always searching but never finding the "now help." God is alive and He uses all different ways to communicate with His beloved ones.

They that hate knowledge and do not choose the fear of the Lord are fools. To which counsel should we incline our ears? The full counsel of the Lord! In these perilous times, people are so in love with themselves. It is so hard for them to receive from others. If we keep ignoring and despising the gifts, God will shut the faucet off on you. I have seen it time and time again. That is a dry land. We need to search out a matter. We need to walk in the fear of the Lord and keep reasoning together, and through the fear of the Lord, search things out. Let deep cry out to His deep, and let wisdom herself guide us with discernment.

The Kingdom of God is Jesus. He ripped His flesh. He opened the heavens, and now He is in us. He went up and sent down His gifts. Sons and daughters shall prophesy. Sons and daughters shall have dreams and visions. It is all biblical. God's dreams never die, never vanish, and never are nonsense. Everybody is trying to listen with their own ears all the time, and sometimes you need to see things through someone's spiritual ears. God says, "He who is spiritual receives the thing of the Spirit, but the carnal do not. Those who are spiritual test and judge all things by the Spirit."

People in the World have more fear of the Lord concerning dreams than people in the church. The king, in **Daniel 2**, cared so much about what he dreamed that he decided to cut in pieces those people who could not interpret his dream. He ended up asking Daniel for help. Pharaoh, another king, needed Joseph to help him to interpret his dream as well. It does not matter your position in the body. We all need each other's gifts. Both of these men were relentless in their pursuit of understanding until they got it. The interpretation of it blessed two nations and saved the kingdoms.

If these two worldly kings were so concerned about their dreams, why do we, the Body of Christ, despise ours? Our gifts will make room for us, but if we despise them, we will miss the places where God wants to take us. The Spirit searches all things, the secret things of God. A lot of people think that dreams are foolish not knowing that some came from God. His sheep hear His voice and another voice they will not follow, even if it is their own voice.

So people end up fearing the dreams and visions more than God and end up quenching the Spirit of God, trusting in man's opinions above the Holy Spirit which is the spirit of wisdom. This is a really serious matter. To despise prophecy is to despise God. All come from His Spirit. God's government will be able to protect us from what comes from man or from darkness. But if you throw the baby away with the bath water, you throw away the opportunity to use the gift of discernment as well and then you will go all the way downhill. We test all things, and in this, we are being led by the Spirit of God, not just by the letter.

What could have happened with Joseph if he had despised a God dream? The angel of the Lord appeared to Joseph, in a dream, telling him about the divine conception (**Matthew 1**). Another angel appeared to Joseph, in a dream, telling him to change his direction (**Matthew 2**). Those who have ears to hear will hear what God is saying through dreams and through visions. The same way God uses His Word, He uses His dreams to edify, to correct, and to rebuke. He knows exactly what He is doing it. And He will do whatever He wants to when He wants to. If we stop harkening to His voice, He will stop talking. Do not quench the Spirit as many denominations have and now are dead. Do not despise prophecy, and pray without ceasing. In doing so, you will tap into His divine protection and His ways.

BREAKING BREAD   1 Thessalonians 5, 1 Corinthians 12:1-21, Proverbs 1, Acts 9:3, Isaiah 11:1-11, Daniel 2, Genesis 41, 1 Corinthians 12, Matthew 1:20-23, Matthew 2:13, Matthew 2:19, Joel 2:28, Jeremiah 23:32, Daniel 1:17, Daniel 7:1-3, Deuteronomy 13:1-3, Numbers 12:6, Zechariah 10:2, Job 33:14-18, 1 Samuel 28:15, Proverbs 18:15-17

"He that hath an ear, let him hear what the Spirit saith unto the churches; To him that overcometh will I give to eat of the hidden manna, and will give him a white stone, and in the stone a new name written, which no man knoweth saving he that receiveth it."

Revelation 2:17

HOPE OF GLORY

God's plan is to fill us with Him. Jesus was fully God and fully man. God wants to fill us continuously with His oil. It is the Glory inside of us that gets people stirred up. People love it or people hate it. The Gospel is about becoming one with Him, and let no man put them asunder. As a man leaves his father and mother, Jesus left His Father's house for His bride, the Church.

Jesus is saying to His bride: Take up your cross. It is your covenant marriage ring. And follow Me. But we can never enter into the kingdom of God unless we become like little children. A child trusts all the time. A lot of us hold onto things. They don't give all to Jesus but they want the blessings. They sacrifice in the flesh, but God wants them to sacrifice in the heart. He wants a circumcised heart where we love God with all of it.

Do we stay as babies or let Christ be formed in us? The World is waiting for the manifestation of this Glory! The Glory shall cover the Earth through His Body. Every tribe and nation, every tongue that called on Jesus and picked up their cross shall call Him their God. Just like Solomon filled the temple with gold, God will fill His temple with His gold, the Glory. Gold represents the Glory, and we now are the temple of God. So, it's Christ in us, the hope of Glory. The Glory in us is the hope of the nations. It is the hope in darkness.

Some people call Him their husband, but they cheat on Him all the time. Because they are not faithful, they can't carry His Glory as His glorious bride. When you are full of His Glory, everybody knows who your husband is. He is the Glory, so you are always with Him. He is always with us, the Glory, the Truth, and the Love. It is all Him. We see many parallels of His exchange. This is the Gospel of the Kingdom.

Everywhere you go, you will see both (Christ and you) walking together. The cross is where we get our new name and identity. Our covenant is in the blood. His Glory is a byproduct of our communion and faithfulness to Him. We cannot be eating at two tables! Just as God divorced Israel and turned them over to Babylon, if we commit adultery with our idols, He will turn us over to the world for the destruction of our flesh and hopefully the saving of our spirit. He said, "Come out from among them. Separate to Him, the Glory of God." We will be a faithful bride.

The hope in Him has to do with trusting and resting in Him. There is no way to be connected to His Glory if we are married (joined) to something else. The invisible God lives inside of us who are born again. He is inside of us. Christ is being formed in us as a seed of incorruption. The manifestation of the sons of God will happen. It is the power of the Gospel unto salvation. So as a man finds his wife, so Jesus finds His bride as the Spirit draws them to Him. He is the head of the church. He is a jealous God so He wants to be in intimate relationship with us, with our heart, mind, and soul. This is where life is. He wants you back in the garden eating from Him. He is the tree of life. Sit under His tree in the shade as it gives fruits in due season and the fruits fall right in your lap as you abide with and in HIM, and you can just eat the fruit. As He covers us in His Glory, we put on Christ. Make no provision for idols and give Him all for all, and this is a great union that God has ordained for us to walk in Him and with Him. So when we are walking in the Spirit, we are sitting at His table.

God put the brain in the head. The head is Christ. The brain should be His. That is the organ that runs the entire vessel as we submit to Him. We live and breathe and have our being. We think like Him, we walk as He walks, so it is with Jesus and the church: walking as one. The two shall become one. It's the most amazing thing, this co-union with Christ. So when we do take communion, it is not just an act. It is real. Bone of His bone. Flesh of His flesh. Spirit of His Spirit. This is the hope we have. Let us have this mind in us: Christ in us – the hope of Glory.

BREAKING BREAD

Mark 10, Ephesians 5, 1 Corinthians 10, Matthew 6, Colossians 1, Romans 8

EAT THE BOOK

In the beginning, we were so free in the garden until we disobeyed God, until we started eating the wrong things. We are always eating, but it is important to know what we eat. Eat the Word of God, you will have life and will feel alive.

On the other hand, you will always feel bad every time you eat what you are not supposed to, just like in the natural when you start getting used to eating healthy and then you eat junk food.

You need to renew your mind by eating the Word. That's why it is so important to pay attention to what we hear because it is what we eat. In His Word, there is no darkness. Everything is pure. You can eat it all. You will never overeat if you do. It will not harm you.

God did not make hell for people. He made heaven for people. He made the garden where there are still two trees. Now we have two tables to eat from: the table of the devil and the table of the Lord. So people choose where they want to go and eat. They will be what they choose to eat. He is the bread of life. The more you eat from Him, the more like Him you are. We need to train ourselves in what we eat. Just like in the natural, we need to consider the devil's table as poison for our spirits.

We still have two trees in the garden. If you still eat from the wrong one, go boldly to Jesus, even when you are ashamed of what you ate. He will purge you, wash you, and restore you!

Give me the book. Give me what I need to eat. You have to be hungry and thirsty. There is only one bread that shall satisfy your spirit. It is the bread of life!

God wants us to be so filled with His Word, to make us as living epistles, a fountain of living water, so when you speak the Word of God, you are speaking as a prophetic voice to the nations because the Word is inside of you.

Get it. Eat it. Chew it. Digest it. A lot of people don't eat the Word but eat everything else. Drink the living water. It causes you to live. The food you eat feeds your spirit. Watch what you eat. How long can you go without food? Without living water? Just like in the natural, you will wither away.

Jesus said His Word is the Living water. It is blood. It is meat. It is His body. There is life in the blood.

People go to church because of the miracles and not for the bread, for all kinds of earthly reasons. We must come together to break bread. We have to seek Jesus so we can live. When Jesus multiplied bread, He had already filled their spirit. He was not as concerned with the natural. He was reminded by the disciples about the natural hunger of the people. Then Jesus fed them naturally and spiritually.

Jesus is the bread that came down from heaven. Since the beginning it was Him, the tree of life, it is Him. The bread of God is Him. He that comes to Jesus shall never hunger or thirst again. If you eat that bread of life, you shall never die. Continuously eat from the tree of life, be clothed by Him. He set before you a table.

Some people will die forever. Some people will live forever. So we all will be around forever either eternal life or eternal death. This is the doctrine of life, if you eat it up you shall surely live!

Jesus said I will give you my flesh. Except you eat Him, receive His blood, His living water, there will not be life in you. This is a hard saying: who can hear this?

God is saying receive it, eat it, chew it. Does the Word of God offend you? But His words are the Spirit and the life. You need to eat it. Religion says: Eat what you want, but the Word of life directs your path. It seems hard but it is not. His yoke is easy and his burden is light. He is asking us to come and eat. Dine with Him. Eat it. Do it. Live it.

You are what you eat. In the kingdom you will become what you eat. You will become like him. Ask: Give me some more bread, some more flesh. Now we know. His words are life, a feast for your spirit.

Did he not choose us? He is everything we need. Without him, nothing was made. Apart from Him, you can't survive. Life or death. Everyday people choose death. Choose life. Choose His bread.

Since the beginning, God had a plan: to redirect us to the tree of life; from it you can eat all. Eat the book! Every single page and the Word will become flesh in you. Let Him encounter you at His table today! Let hunger and thirst be your ambition! That will bring you back to His table. Then you will be eating daily His book, our daily bread! Eat the book and live!

Shane W Roessiger

BREAKING BREAD

John 1:1-17, Genesis 2, Genesis 3, Revelation 10:7-11, John 6

TRUTH NOT FOR SALE

WWW.HOTHOUSEOFTRUTH.COM

All books published by H.O.T. HOUSE OF TRUTH are free of charge and of leaven.

H.O.T. House of Truth – Apostolic Center

360 S Tamiami Trail – Nokomis – FL – (941) 412-5414

Equipping the Saints – Sending them out